Purse Universe

Portraits of women and their purses
from *The Purse Project*

Book design by Tim Kolankiewicz

Published by Crane Hill Publishers
www.cranehill.com

Printed in Italy

Library of Congress Cataloging-in-Publication Data

Hagerty, Barbara G. S.
Purse universe / Barbara G.S. Hagerty.
p. cm.
ISBN 1-57587-176-9
1. Portrait photography. 2. Handbags—Pictorial works. 3. Handbags—Anecdotes. I. Title.

TR680 .H245 2001
391.4'4—dc21

2001047008

Visit the Purse Universe website at www.barbarahagerty.com

10 9 8 7 6 5 4 3 2 1

For my pal Gail
Old friends are best!
XOXOXO
Barbara G. S. Hagerty

Purse Universe

Portraits of women and their purses from *The Purse Project*

Barbara G.S. Hagerty

CRANE HILL
PUBLISHERS

Introduction

The idea for this book began two years ago with two columns I wrote for *Skirt!* magazine, exploring purses and the people—usually females—who carry them. Everything about purses intrigues me, beginning with their paradoxical qualities: They're public yet private, practical yet symbolic, universal yet individual.

More than a mere utilitarian container, a purse can be an incarnation of the person who carries it—a miniature portrait or autobiography in cloth, beads, plastic, feathers, or vinyl. It is object, symbol, totem, and metaphor. It guards secrets and betokens femininity and fecundity. It is guarded carefully and held intimately next to the body. It is like another appendage, extra body part, third bosom, third eye, small womb, portable inner sanctum, or alter ego.

After those two columns I realized I had only begun to explore the theme. So I began to document purses and their owners through 35mm black-and-white photography, a body of work that would become an exhibit called *The Purse Project*. At this juncture I made a wonderful discovery that constitutes the heart and soul of *The Purse Project*: Indeed there is a relationship between a female and her purse that is personal, deeply felt, and unique as the individual herself. The purse is an attachment, an involvement, an identification.

Although I'd seen articles over the years about the contents of women's purses, I'd never seen a work exploring them in their complex, highly charged totality. Women, I quickly learned, were eager to talk about their purses and to articulate on the subject in general. As one woman said to me, "I've been waiting my whole life for someone to ask me about my purse."

Thus I began to interview my purse portrait subjects, editing their spoken narratives down to the bare essence and placing them with the photographs. These narratives take various forms, including anecdote, rationale, history, purse theory, and even anti-purse theory. Sometimes "the story" is the purse's contents, but more often it's the total purse—its physical, metaphysical, or historical qualities. The common thread is the intensity and particularity of identification the owner feels with this most indispensable of belongings.

Each portrait is of a real person, pictured with the purse she actually uses, whether daily or occasionally. I have found my portrait subjects in every conceivable way: through word of mouth, serendipity, publishing my telephone number and an ad in *Skirt!*. I even stopped strangers on the street in Charleston and on my travels.

When I describe *Purse Universe*, I tell people to think of books portraying dogs and their owners. On one level, this is "Purses and their Owners." On another, it is about the joy, whimsy, and poignance conveyed by a universal object and the amazing universe of people who carry it.

—Barbara G.S. Hagerty
Charleston, South Carolina

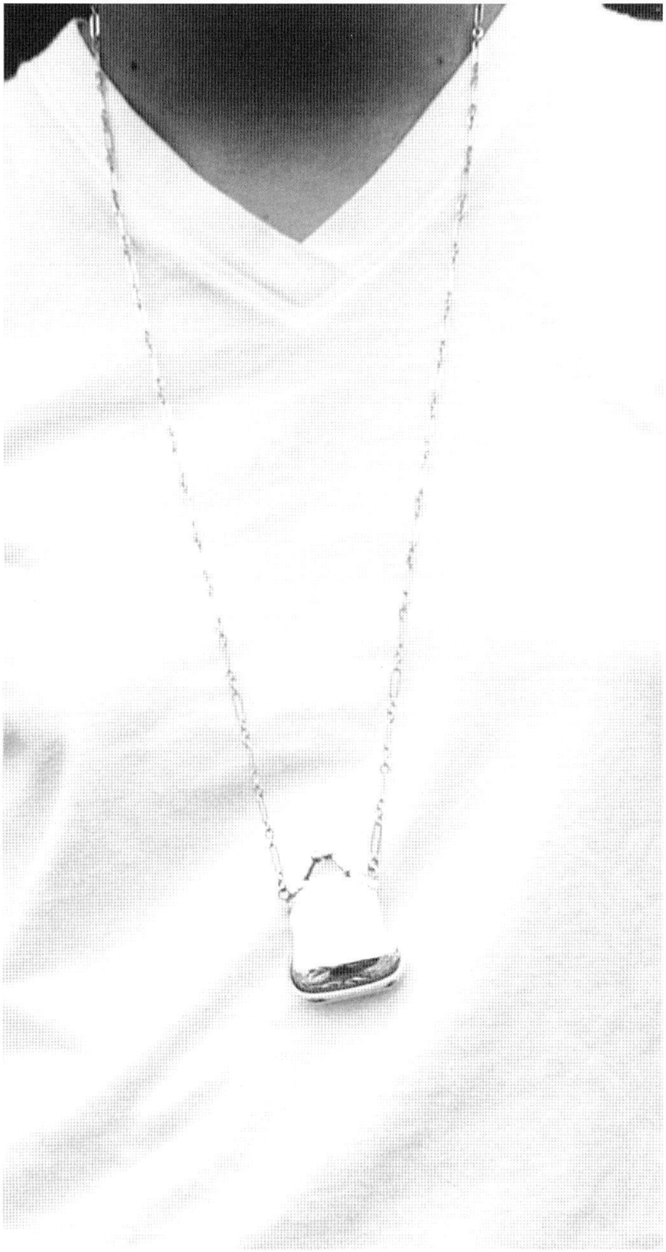

Purse Metaphysics

Carried or worn,
gigantic or minute,
a female's purse
packs potent symbolism.
It's adornment or jewel,
small womb, third eye,
intimate icon, portrait
in miniature, the body's
other solar plexus.

Marcia Warnock
Purse Theorist

The Right Purse

I've been waiting my whole life for someone to ask me about my purse. I carry mine a minimum of ten years. This one still has a little life left in it. When my last oldie but goodie disintegrated, I searched and searched 'til I found this one. It's got to hit the hip in a certain place, and have a certain number of sections. It's got to have the right strap.

The very first time I carried it, at eight in the morning, Cheryl van Landingham said, "Marcia, you have a new purse!"

Once in a while I go through my purse like Colin Fletcher, the backpacker who wrote the book on how to get the load down. He cut labels off underpants and handles off toothbrushes.

Every now and then I shave the load down, getting rid of a key or a few papers, 'til nothing extraneous is left except a mint wrapper or the tooth of a comb.

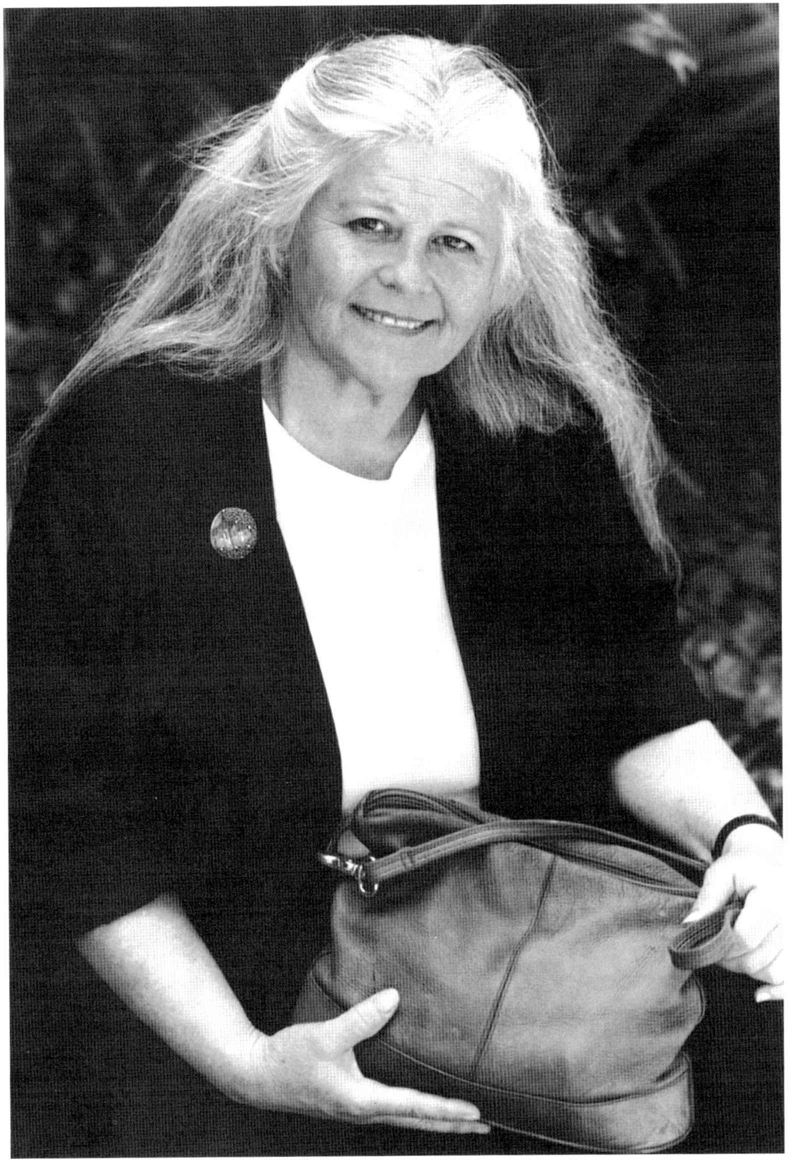

Zera Marvel

Rock Musician

Cat Bag

I have a day job stuffing potpourri into sachets. At night I sing with the rock group Tagging Satellites. We just made our first CD, *Shooting Down the Airwaves.*

I make costumes, clothes, and headdresses. I'm always looking everywhere—in thrift shops, flea markets, even on the sidewalk—for knickknacks, beads, and other interesting things. I decorated my pocketbook with two trinkets I got from gumball machines: a miniature gun and a sticker of a cat with a nose ring.

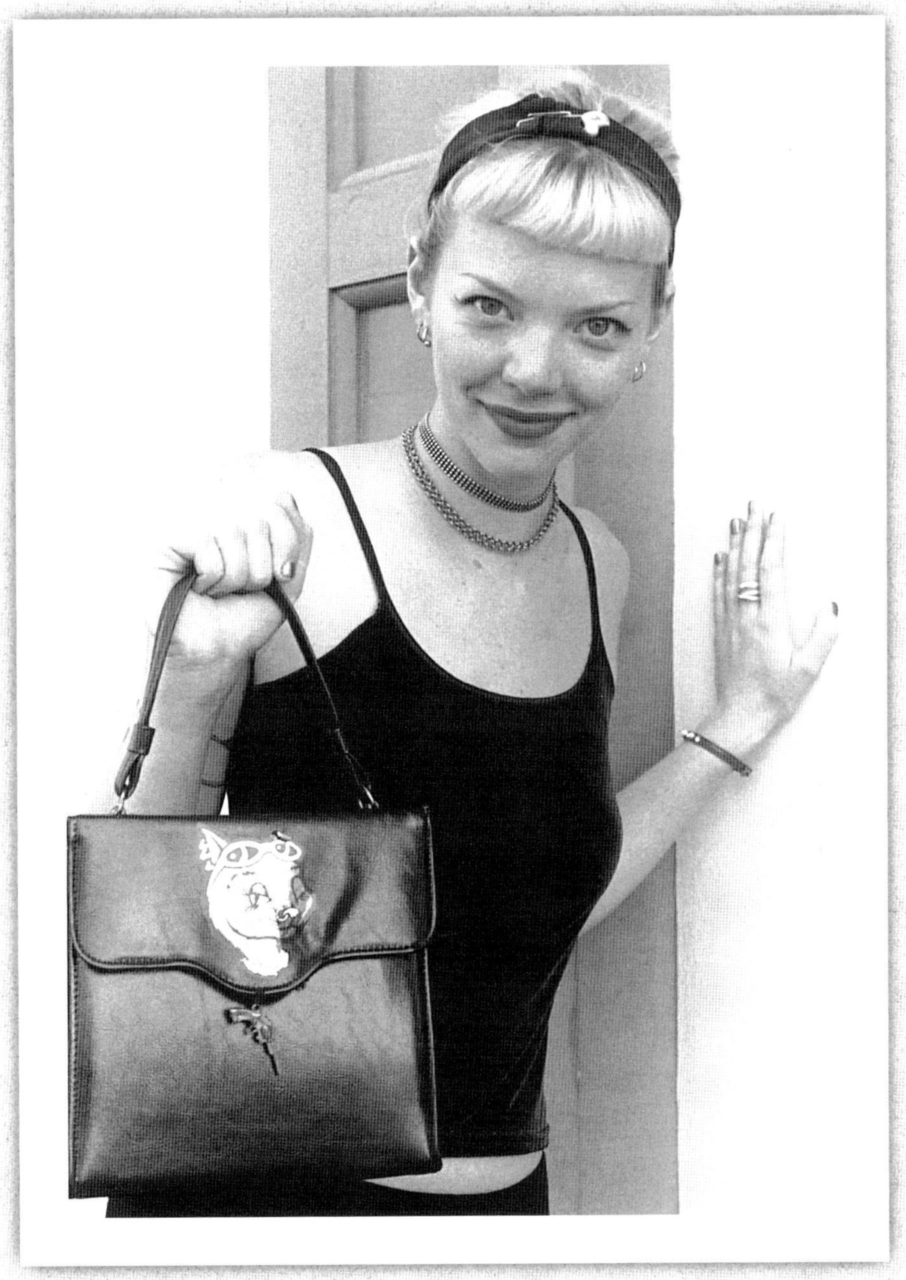

Torreah "Cookie" Washington

Designer and Owner of "Phenomenal Women"

Just a "Bag"

Born in Morocco.

Couturiere extraordinaire and inventor of the Kiss Purse.

My dear, sweet Grandma carried a pocketbook.

My sophisticated mother carried a handbag.

I carry simply a bag.

And my beautiful young daughters think

that all purses are book bags.

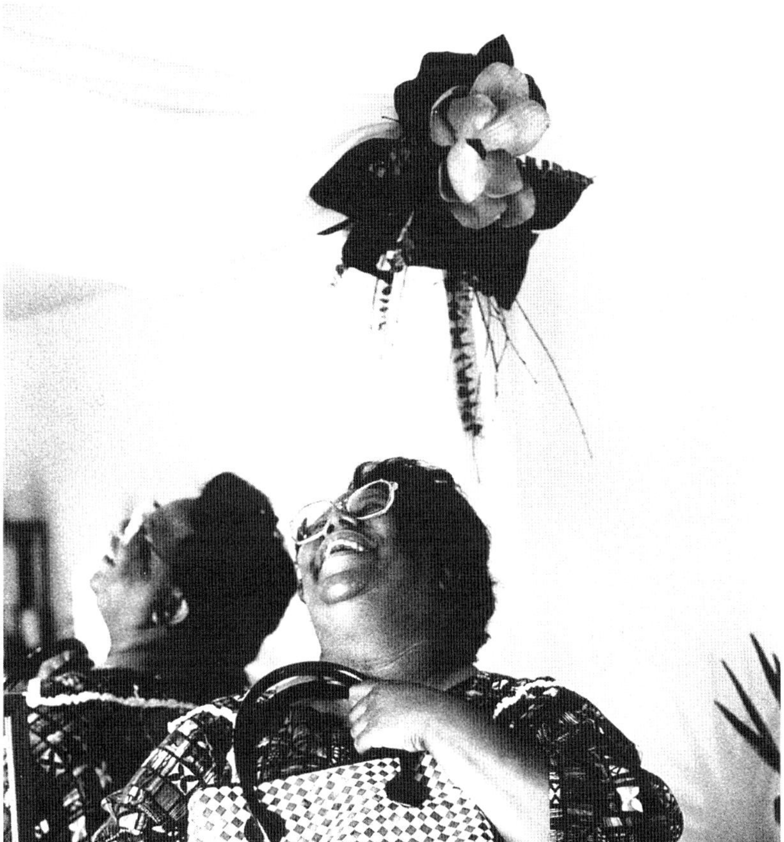

Mahala Eden Fonvielle

Waitress, Tap Dancer

Tolerance

I'm like Tank Girl, the anti-heroine of the comic book and movie. I'm a firm believer in being prepared. Tank Girl is assertive and can kick ass, if needed.

I never leave home without at least two shopping bags. I've always got water with me and something to eat—an orange, pear or banana. I carry Band-Aids, Mace, my journal, bus fare, my calming tea (you can tell I'm high-strung), and B vitamins. And something to read, comic books or feminist 'zines. If I ever need to run away, I'm ready.

My degree is in psychology, but I burned out on it after six years of school and waitressing. I'm thinking of going to naturopathic school.

I like to tap dance. And I have an amazing monkey call.

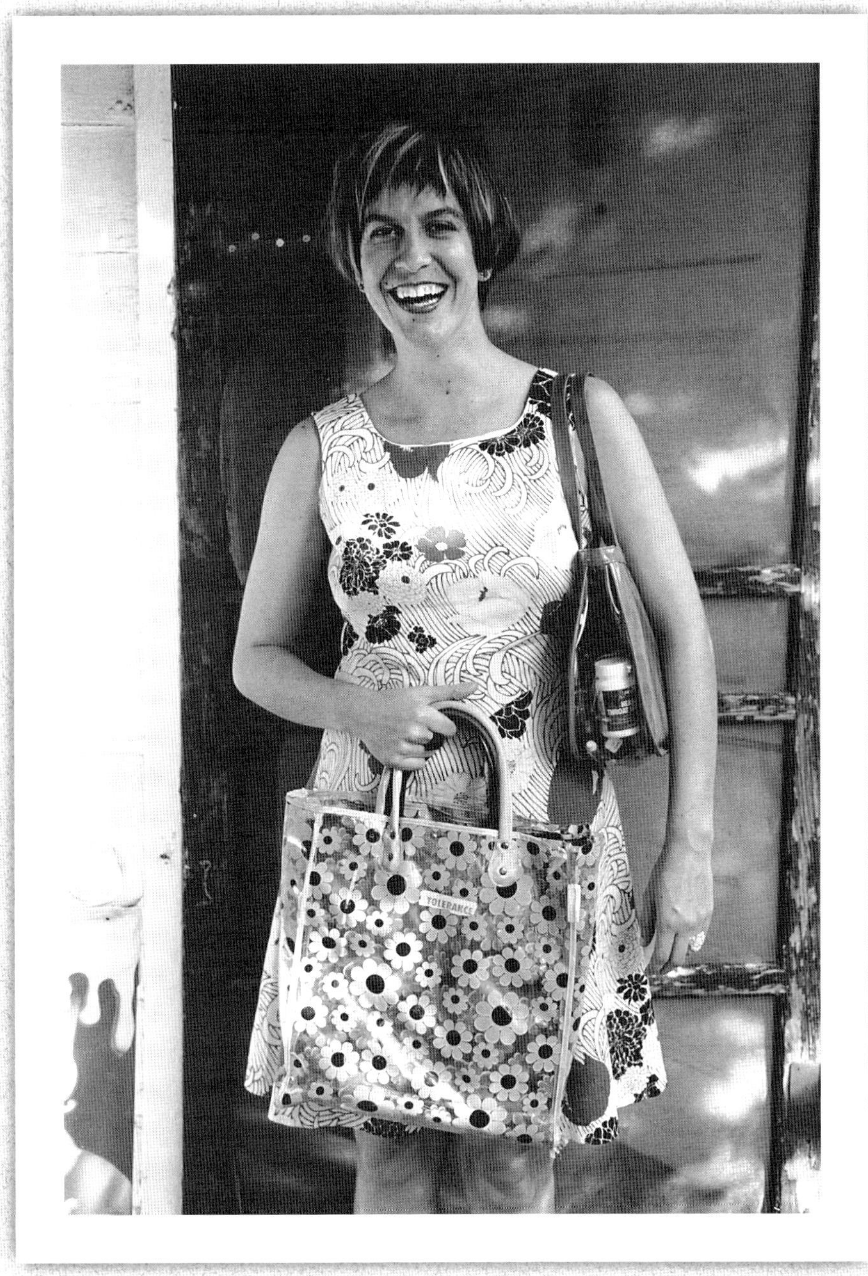
TOLERANCE

Becky Bright
Barbie Collector

Barbie Lunch Kits

Hello. My name is Becky Bright. These are my Barbie lunch kits that lead the double life of carryall handbags.

I am a Barbie collector. As you may see, I don't believe all that rot about Barbie lowering a girl's self-esteem. I feel quite special when I carry my bags, thank you very much.

My aspirations are to draw lots of stuff, take lots of pictures, and write everything down.

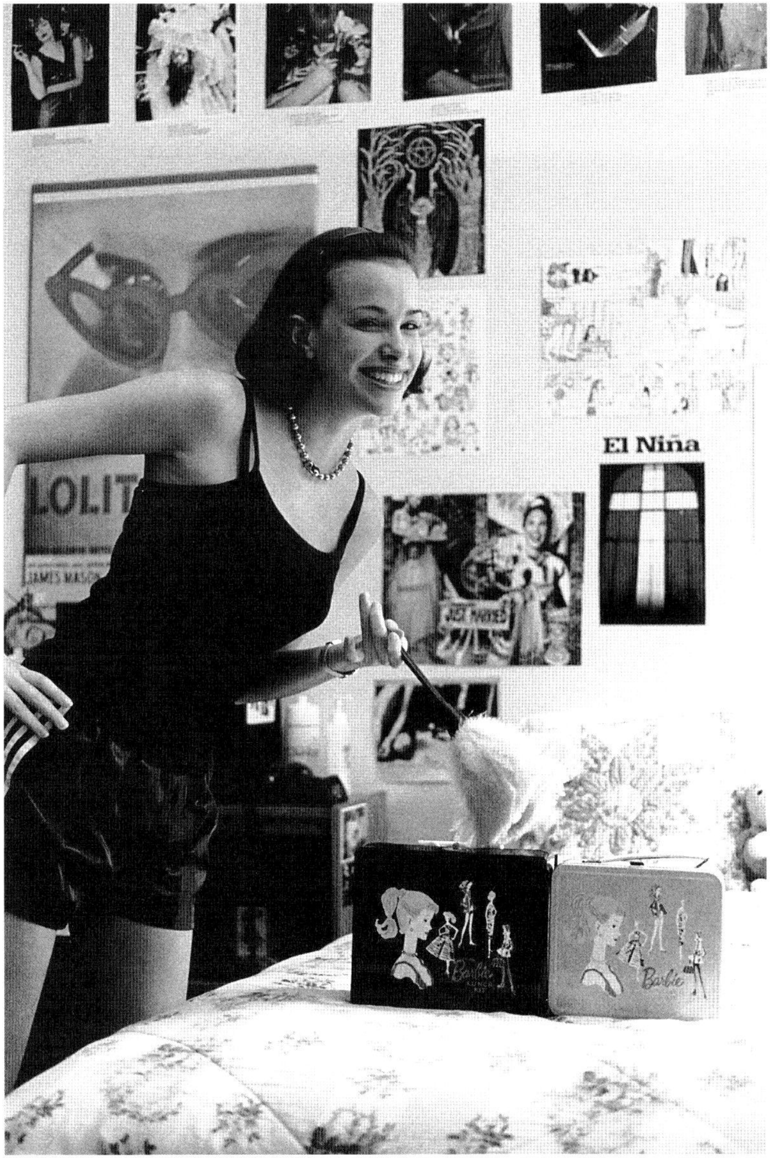
El Niña
LOLIT
Barbie

Mariana Hay and Mary Loretta Croghan Ramsay

Granddaughter and Grandmother

Television Purse and Titanic Purse

I love to collect pocketbooks. I have pocketbooks from all sorts of places. When I was little I would pack them up with junk. I have so many I always forget where I put them. Pocketbooks are great!

—Mariana Hay *(left)*

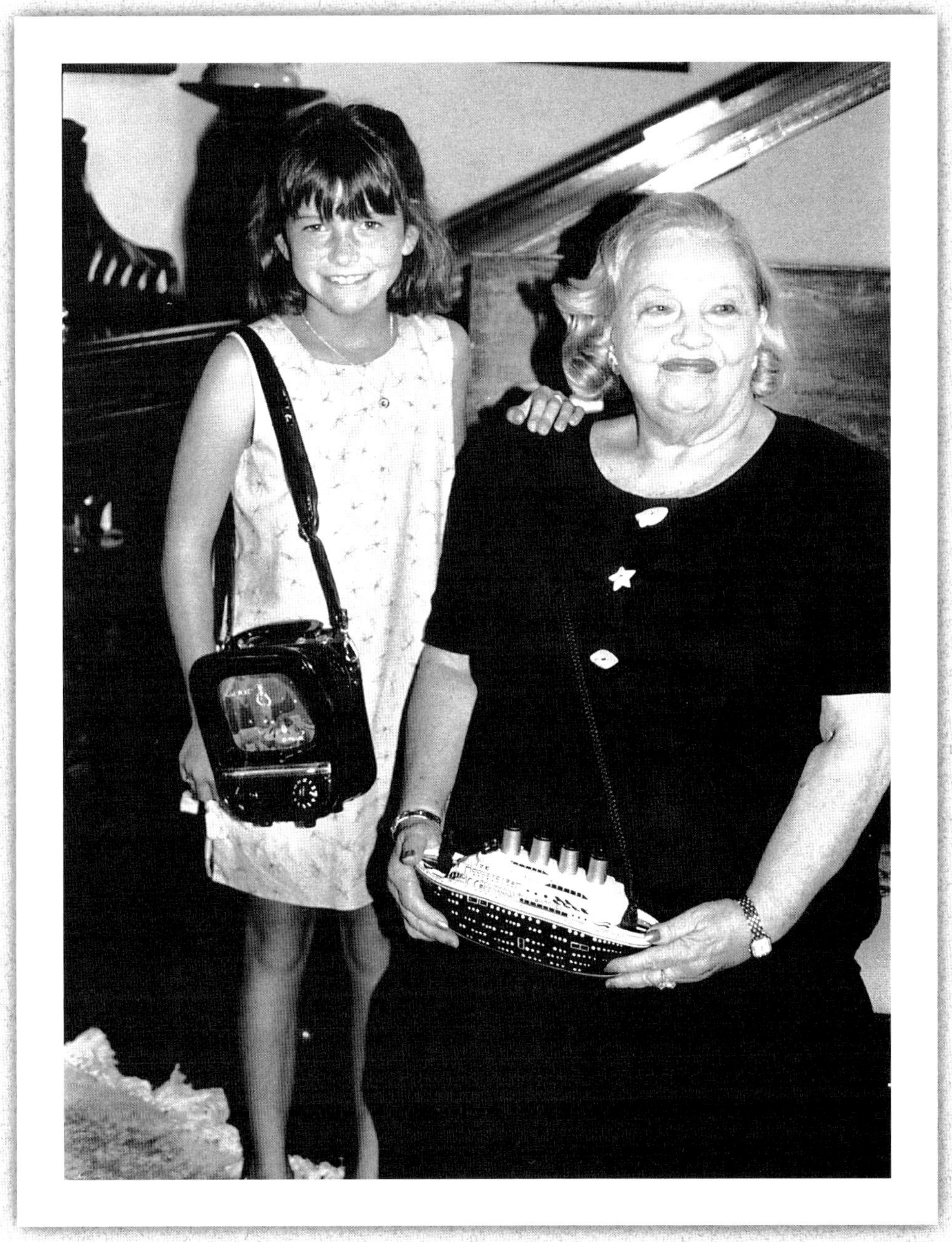

Maureen Myers
Travel Agent

Jingle Jangle Purse

A purse like this one is worn to attract the male species. That's been forgotten—or it's not "PC" to say it.

With a purse like this, you get a lot of extra attention. This is what you want. You are a single woman. Anything that gets people to look at you is helpful.

This purse is a conversation piece. Based on my psychological history as an only child with a fear of rejection, I have no concept of flirting. The purse is a ploy, that aspect of fashion to attract men, or to be one up on your girlfriends.

Accessories have a seductive quality: purses, shoes, and hats always fit. You don't have to go on a diet. They're a shtick. They get people to talk to you.

I once had a girlfriend who stuck a black feather in the back of each shoe. Can you imagine? Wooooo!!!

This purse is a hook, as if to say, "Look at me. Talk."

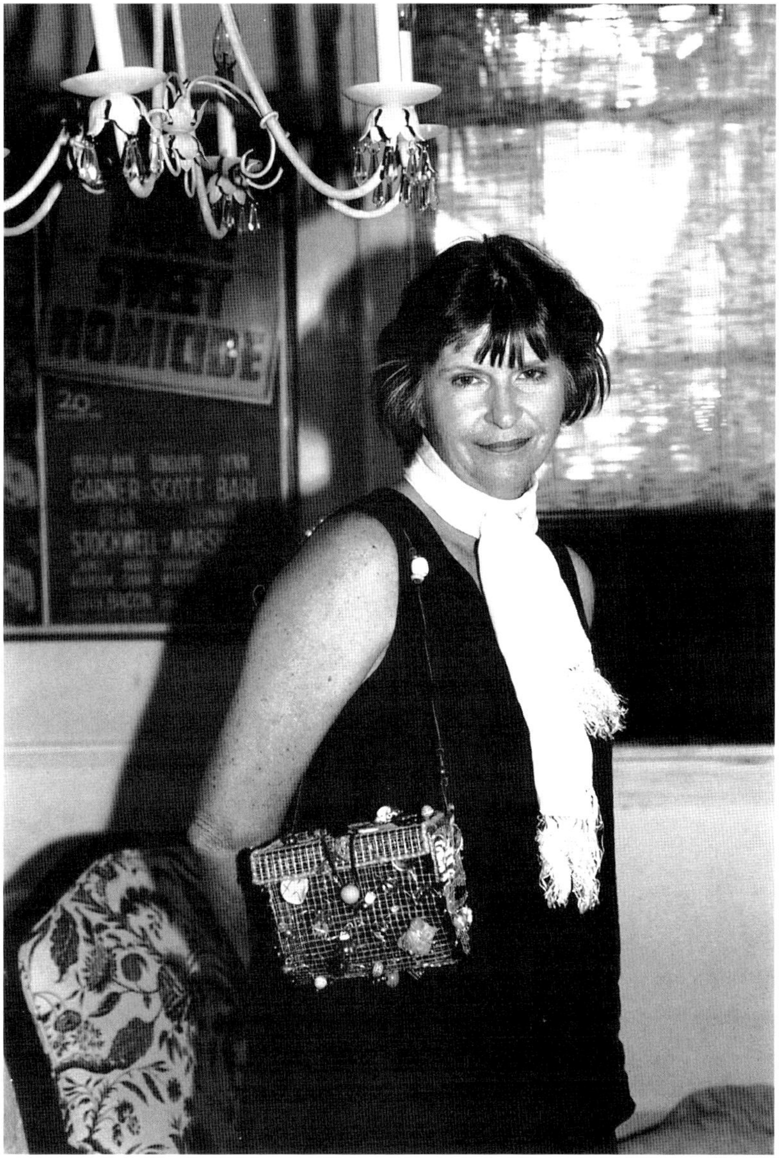
SWEET
HOMICIDE

Africa

Drag Queen

Leather Purse

Name: Africa

Age: Ageless

Gender: Every

Occupation: Bimbo

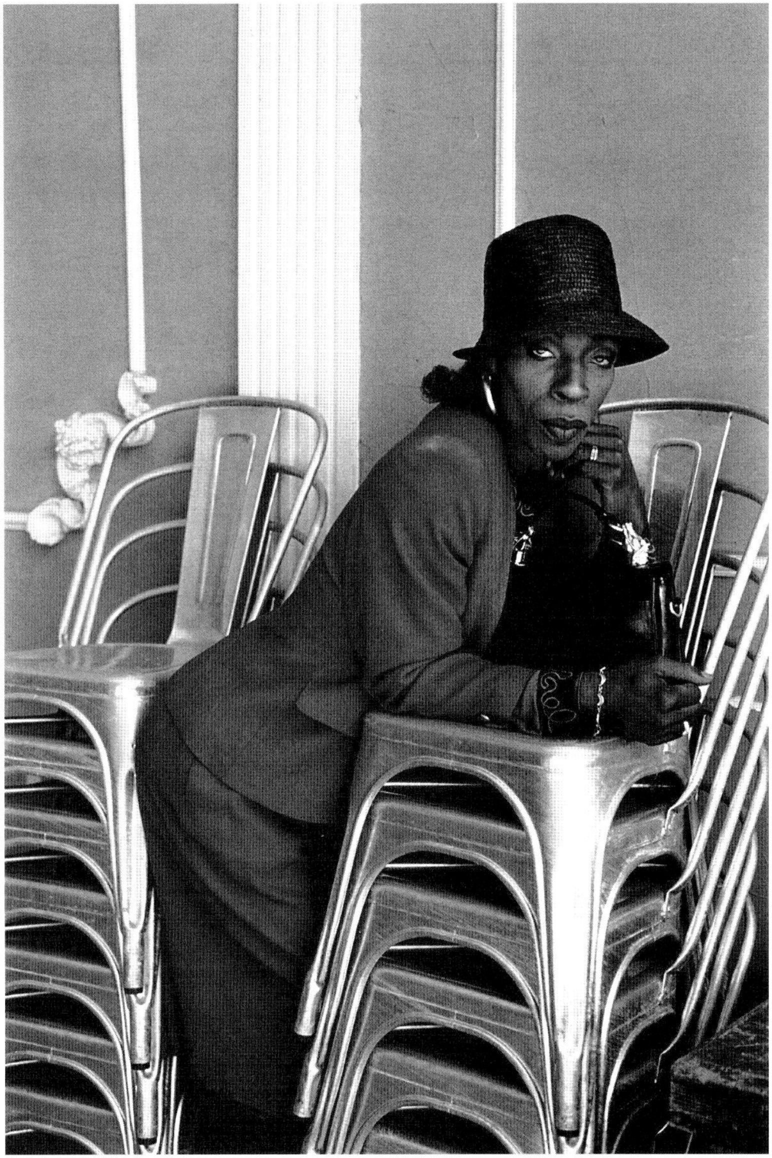

Arla Holroyd and Virginia Neyle

Retired Teacher and Realtor

Church Purses

I was born in 1917 and reared to attend church in proper attire. You NEVER went without stockings, gloves, a hat, and a purse.

Here I am in my Barbara Bush pearls, plain pearl earrings, and lavender straw hat.

In my church purse I keep my offering, handkerchief, a tube of lipstick, and Arsenicum Album, a refined derivative of arsenic, for my asthma, just in case. I also have my crucifix with Jesus and my miraculous medals. I carry a medal of the Blessed Mother, which is a replica of the one my husband carried during World War II in the Pacific. She protected him and he did not get a scratch. I also carry the medallion of St. Jude, the Patron Saint of Impossible Causes.

—Virginia Neyle *(right)*

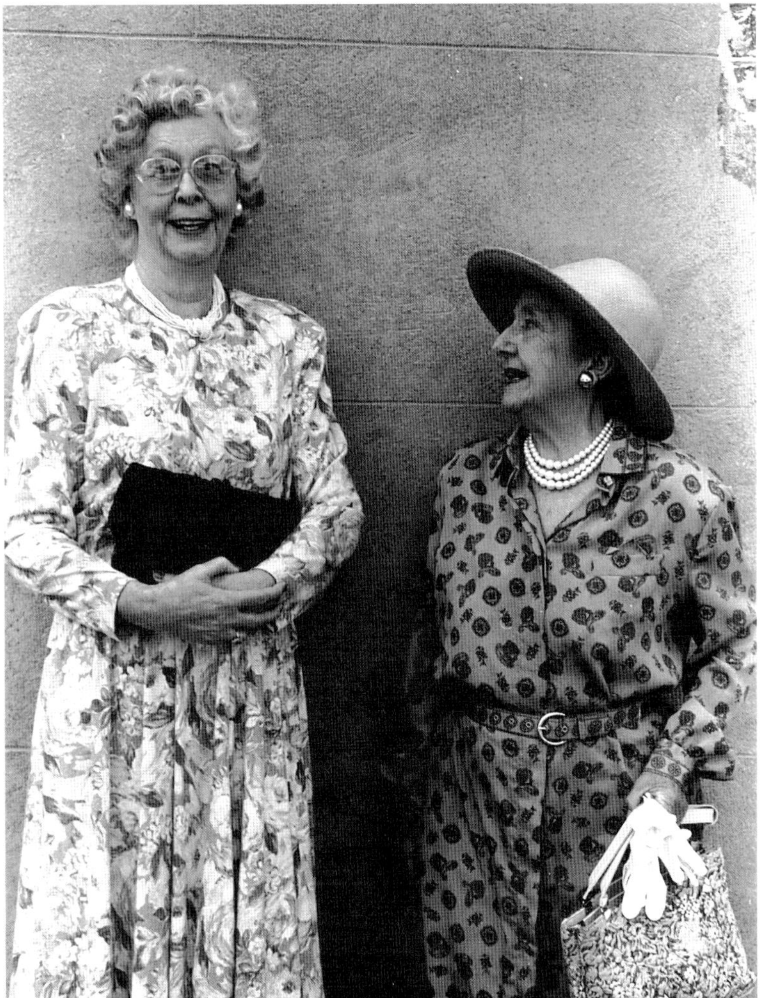

Kathleen Millat Johnson

Artist

"Hand" Bag

I am a playful person. Among other projects, I've created some life-size, soft sculptures of my grandparents. Sometimes my husband Nick and I play with them, hide one or the other in the bed and pull back the covers.

When I created these soft sculptures—using queen-size panty hose and cotton batting—I had some body parts left over. I like the play on words of "hand" bag, and so I made myself this purse. Just wait until I do a "shoulder" bag.

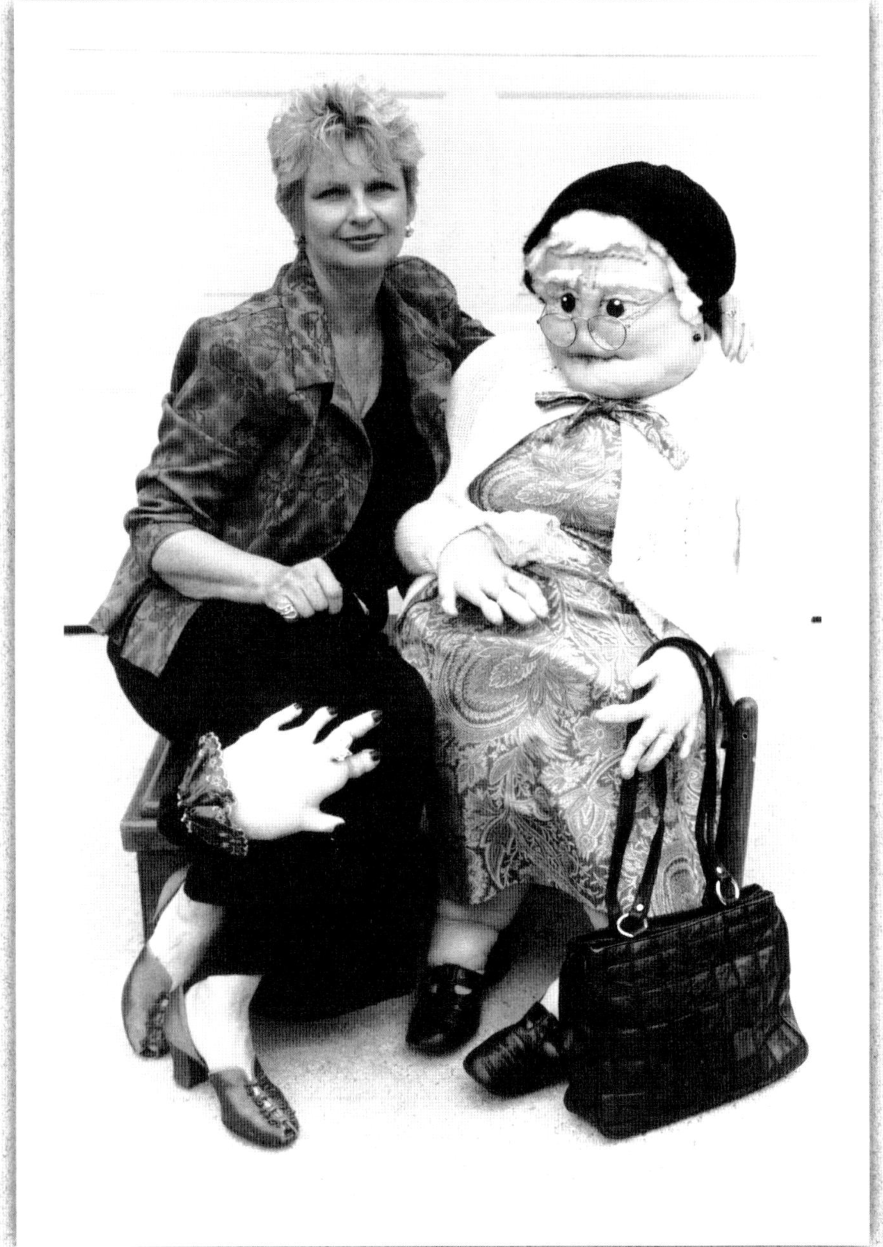

Chaunee Grimsley
United States Air Force

African Purse with Fish and Pennies

I am a wanna-be writer. I've got my fingers crossed and am trying to get up the nerve to submit a short story for publication. Oh, I'm not just crossing my fingers. I'm going to do it.

My family is from Wadmalaw Island, South Carolina, where rice was grown. We have been in this country about two hundred years. We may be from Sierra Leone. But the continent of Africa is vast, and unless you want to do an Alex Haley and go through slave records . . . Instead, I want to embrace it all. That makes more sense. It would be too all-consuming for me to seek out my individual past. I'm just me. I'm an American.

My aunt is a traveling woman. She bought this fabric—very African in feel and color—and left it at our house for about a year. I thought I'd make a purse out of it. I don't think she's coming back for it.

The whole vibe of the bag feels African to me. I relate to the fish because I love the water. I glued the copper pennies on with Krazy Glue, and they stay on well as long as I don't bang into something. I wanted my bag to have pizazz. I like the way it catches light. And I'll never be broke. I'll never be penniless.

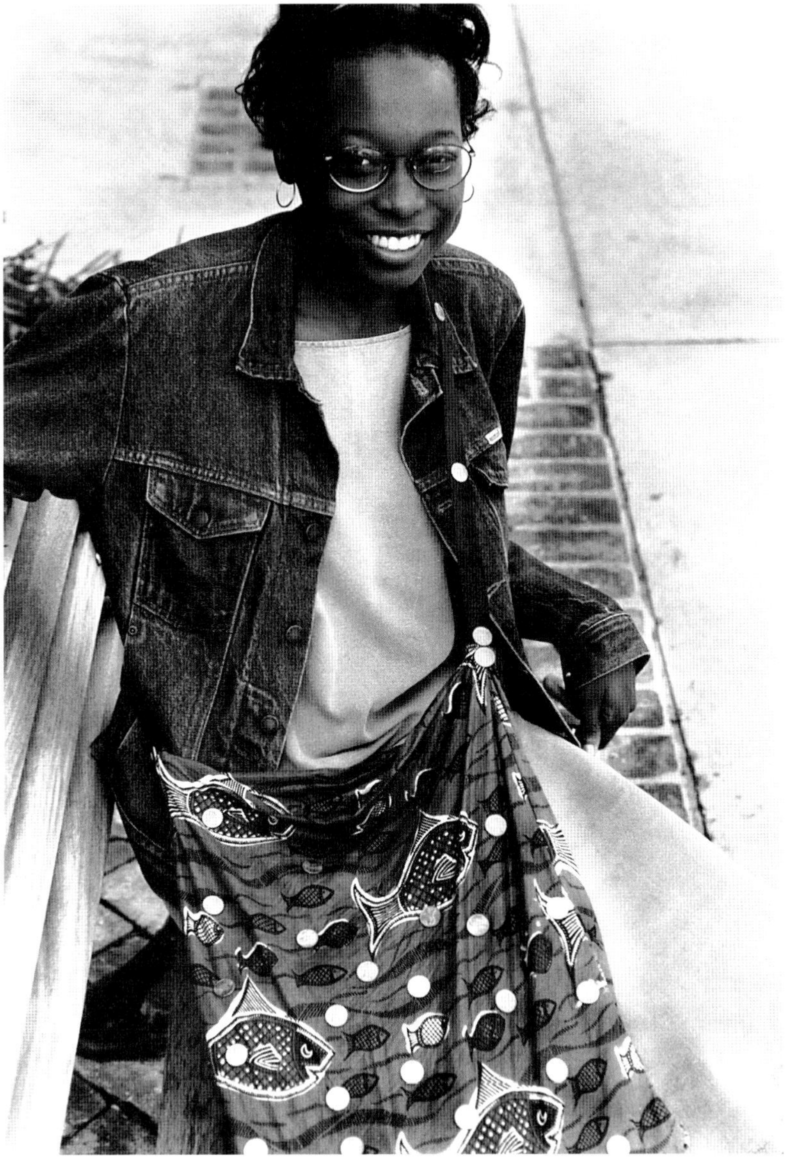

Hayley and Sally
Junior Purse Connoiseurs

Smiley Face Purse and White Plastic Purse

My grandmother gave me the Smiley Face purse when I went to visit her in Chattanooga because she was really happy to see me. I call her "Susie"—not Grandmother Susie—just regular Susie.

I keep my sunglasses, jewelry (some plastic, some real), and makeup inside. I have fake lipstick and fake nail polish. Also some real money, and tissues that I pretend are handkerchiefs.

—Hayley Hunt *(left)*

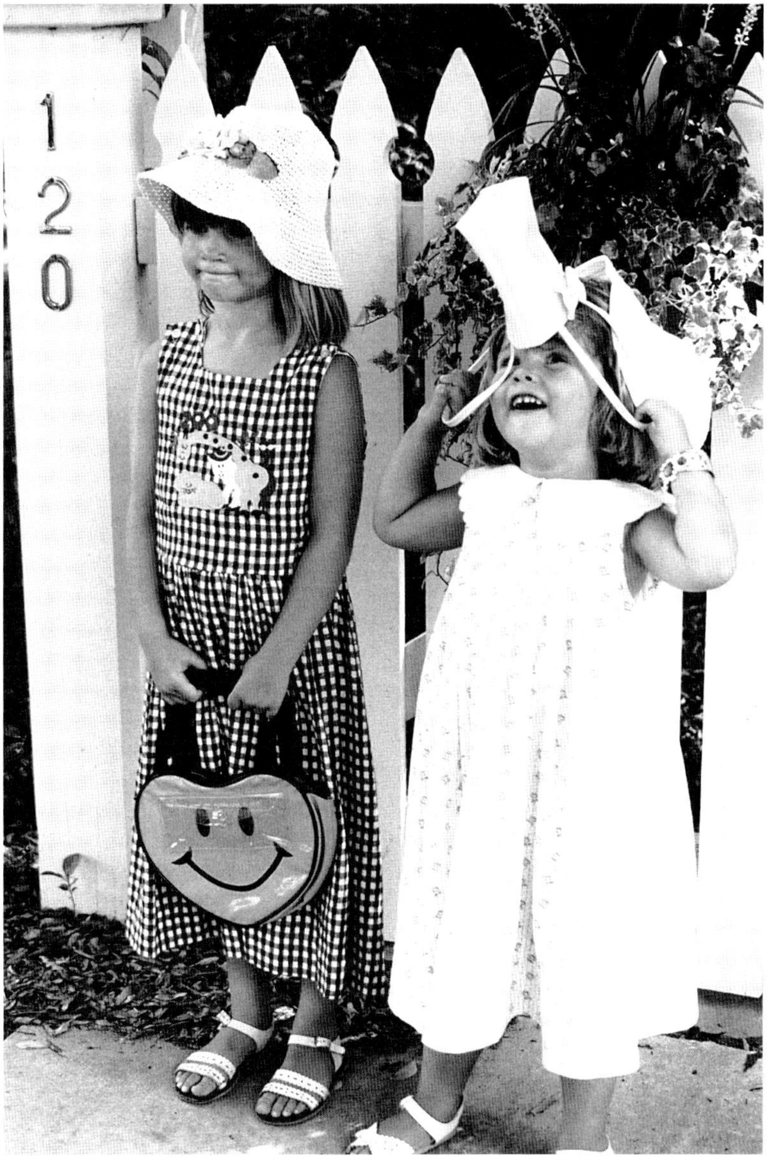
120

Suzannah Simmons
Student

Unisex Symbol Backpack, A Political Billboard

Outwardly, the symbol on my backpack looks like a unisex bathroom sign. To me, however, it represents the equality of the sexes. We are male and female, separate, different, equal. The symbol embodies both appreciating our differences and remembering we have yet to achieve full equality on every level.

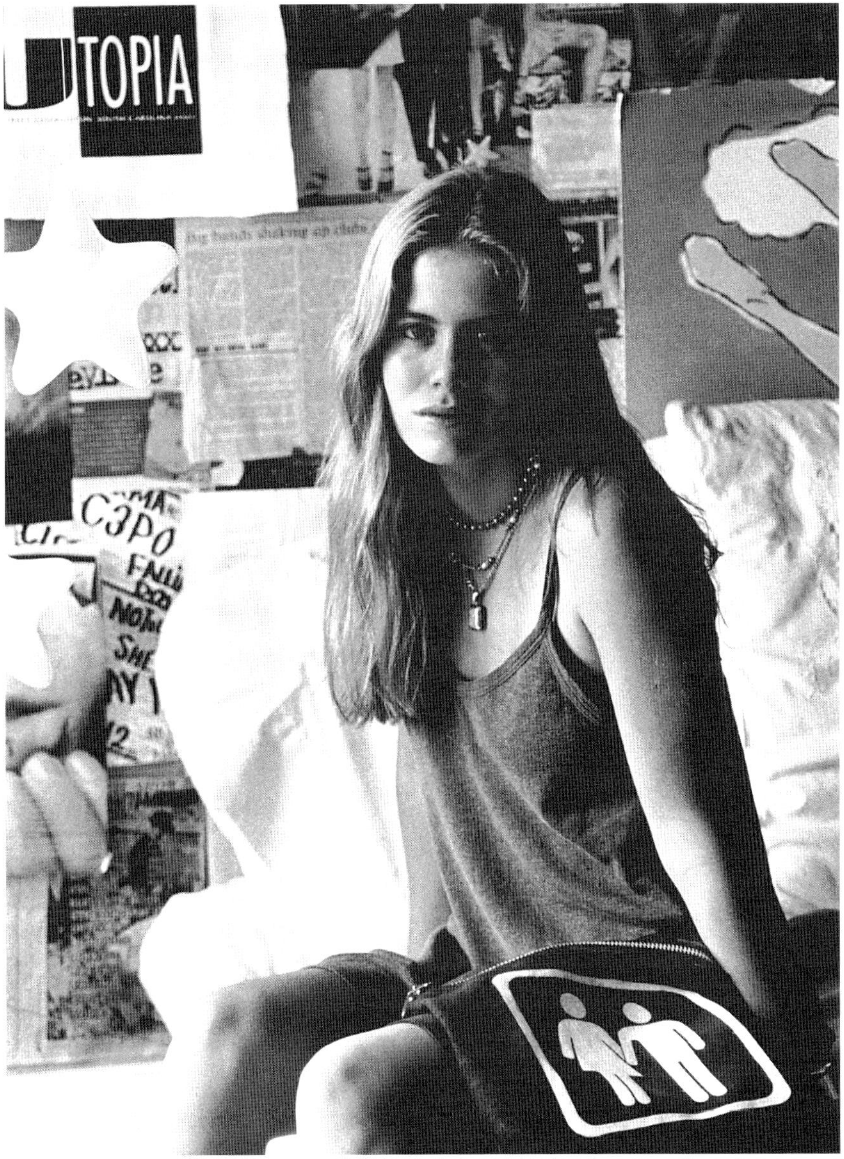
UTOPIA

Jane Nepveux
Retired Teacher

Barn Purse

I carried this little red barn purse with me during my twenty years as a substitute teacher. It was just me—my tag, my personality.

When children saw me coming with that bag, they saw me as a friend. This was no foe. Someone who loved them was approaching.

It's on a shelf in the den now. Inside is a letter from my superintendent, thanking me for my years of service, and other mementos.

I wish I still had every letter from those children who wrote me and said, "Thank you for being my teacher." I wish I had a picture of every single child I taught those years.

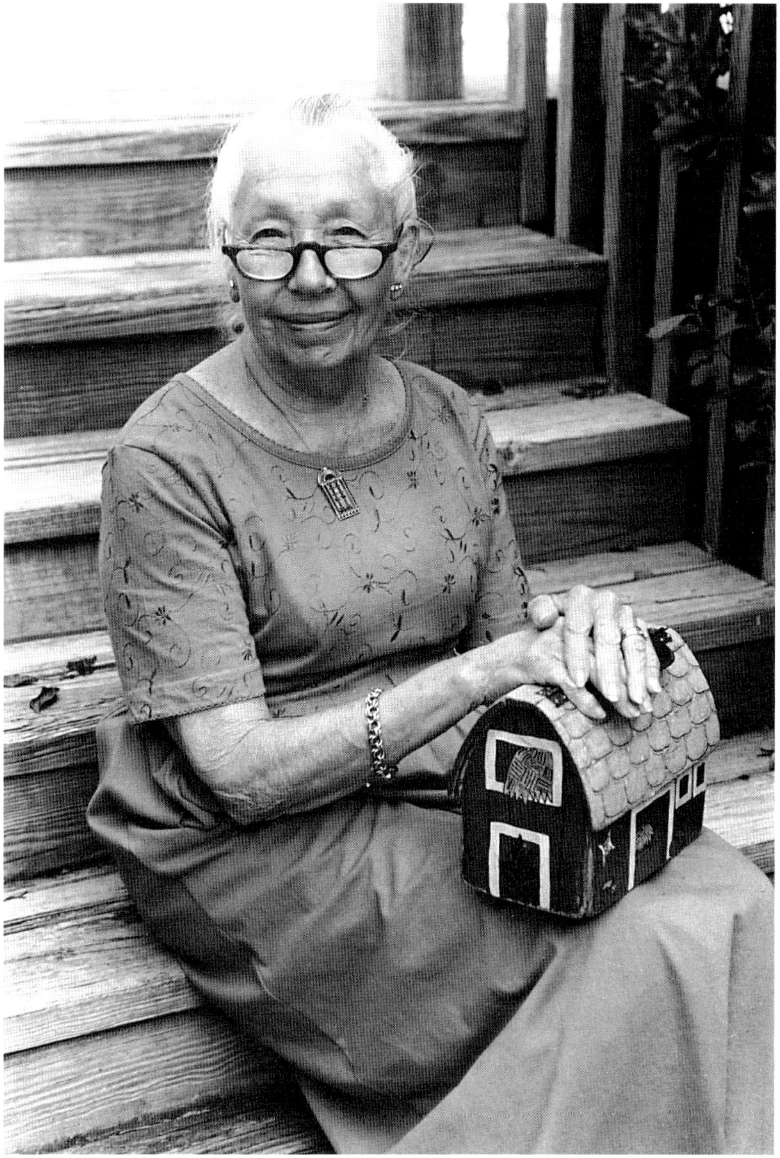

Wendy Marcus Goer
Interior Designer

Baseball Evening Purse

I wanted something special to wear to my middle son's bar mitzvah. Since his date was assigned two years in advance, I had ample time to get all aspects of his major Life Cycle Event organized. On a trip to New York City, I spotted the baseball evening bag in a jewelry store off Fifth Avenue. Its price tag was more than I wanted to afford, so I left it there.

For weeks though . . . I kept thinking about it and finally rationalized that it would be the "jewelry" that I would wear for Kenzie's celebration dinner dance. I wanted to reflect his sparkle as a principled person and his passion for the all-American game of baseball.

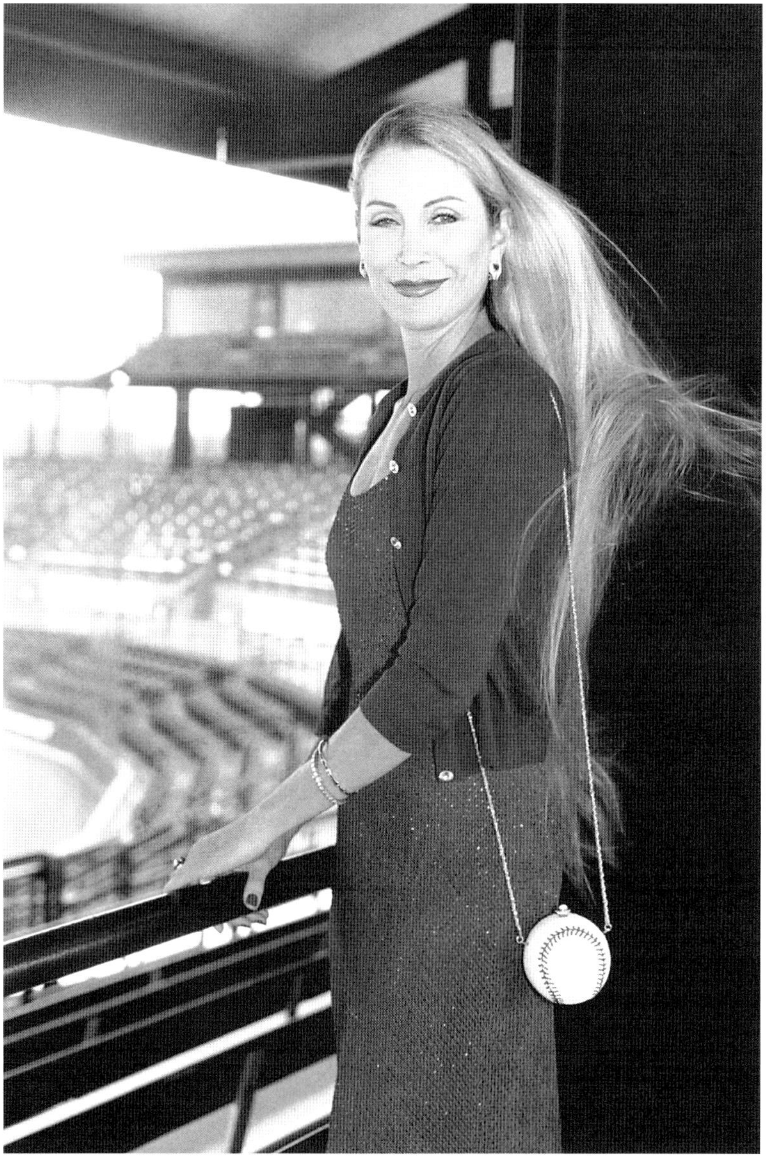

Robin Shuler
Category Defier

Tillye's Purse

I have no category. I'm an actress, playwright, and founder of the Pluffmud Club. My most recent role was Nurse Ratched in *One Flew Over the Cuckoo's Nest.*

This was my Grandma Tillye's purse. She was kind of a butterball on wheels. A real bitch who never minced words. I loved her so much I named my daughter after her.

When she died, the family divided her things up. I just stood to the side and waited. What was not taken was what I wanted—her appliances, costume jewelry, and this pocketbook.

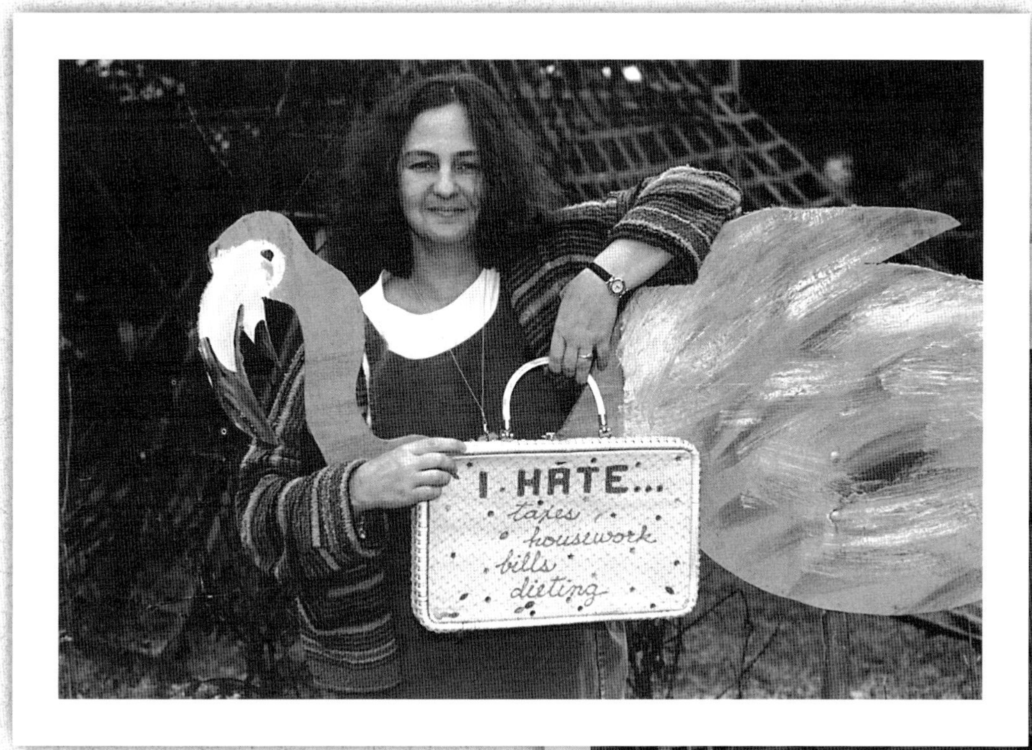
I HATE...
taxes
housework
bills
dieting

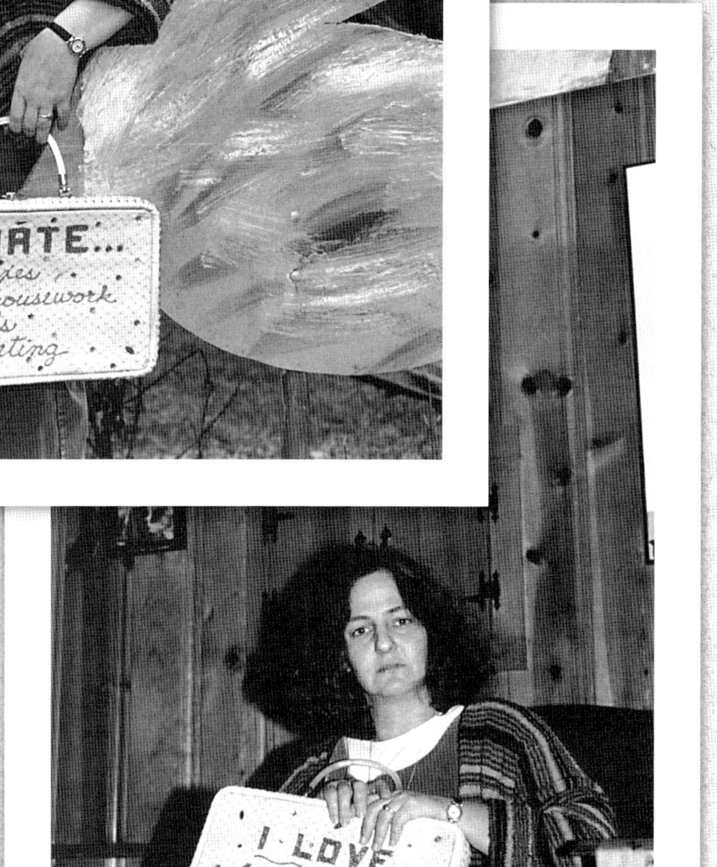
I LOVE...
vacations
mink
parties
diamonds

Mimi Funderburke

Artisan

Beaded Turtle Shell Evening Bags

I make jewelry and purses from stones and bones, animal hides, discarded things, and natural objects. These evening bags I make by beading or by gold- or silver-leafing the shells of farm-raised turtles. Otherwise, the shells would go to waste.

Indigenous peoples have been using turtle shells for hundreds of years as containers, smudge pots, and as something to hold things.

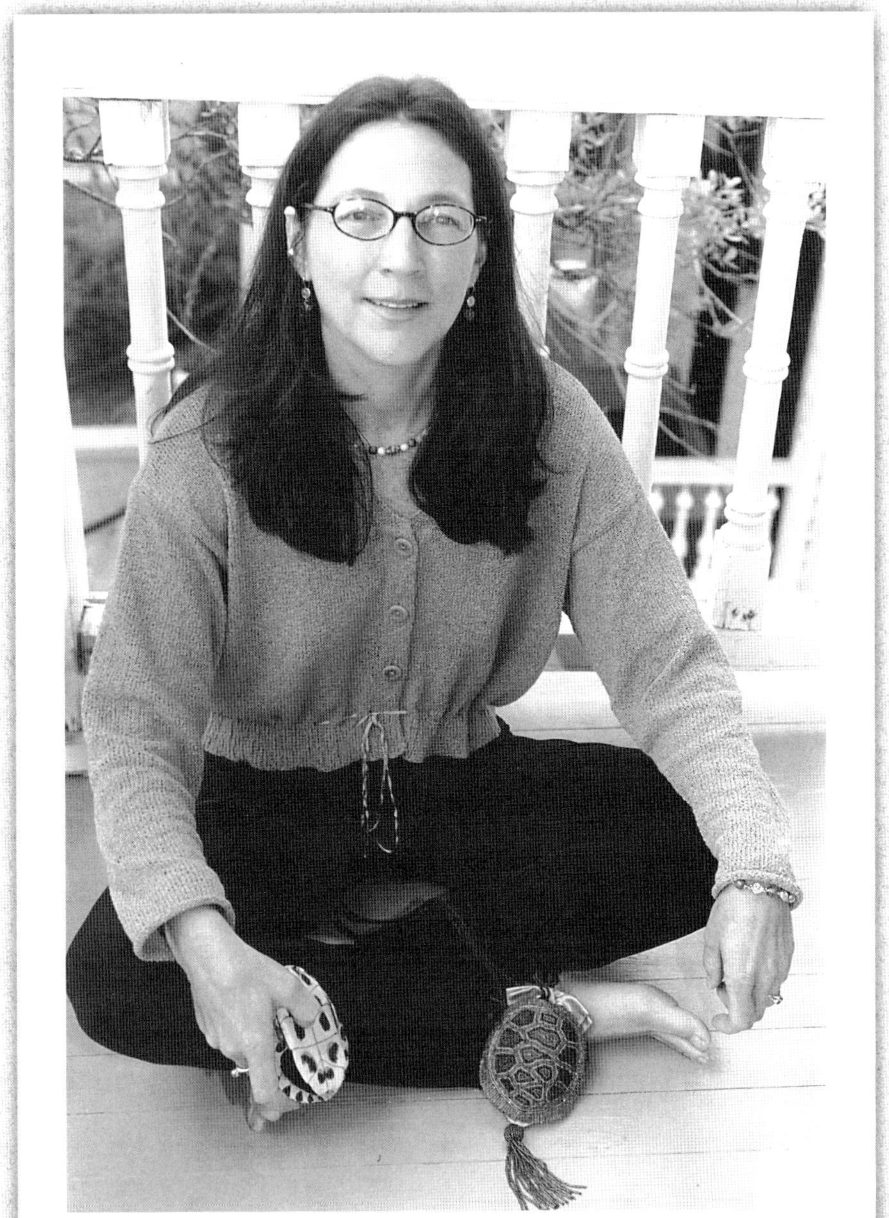

Diane Hamrick, Ph.D.

Psychotherapist

Purse on Wheels

I've always used my car as a motorized purse. It helps me as I transition from place to place. I long ago outgrew the confines of a traditional purse.

The car is a purse, and there are many purses within the purse. As is my exterior manifestation so is my interior manifestation. I have compartments within compartments within my psyche. So I climb into my mechanical purse.

These are the compartments within: 1. Mediation Bag 2. Psychodiagnostic Tool Bag (Rorschach and IQ tests) 3. Grandmother's Bag (change of clothes, toothpaste, modeling clay) 4. Glove Compartment (tapes and directions to Most Favorite Places) 5. Real Purse (for when I have to look together) 6. my Magic Rock (on dashboard).

Women's bellies contain babies, and for them cars are most useful as containers that protect. Both cars and purses represent the placenta. Both are home, nest, womb, container, transitional object, nourishing what might be.

Whereas for men, cars represent the ego, the peacock feathers, a status symbol. What's under the hood is what's in the pants.

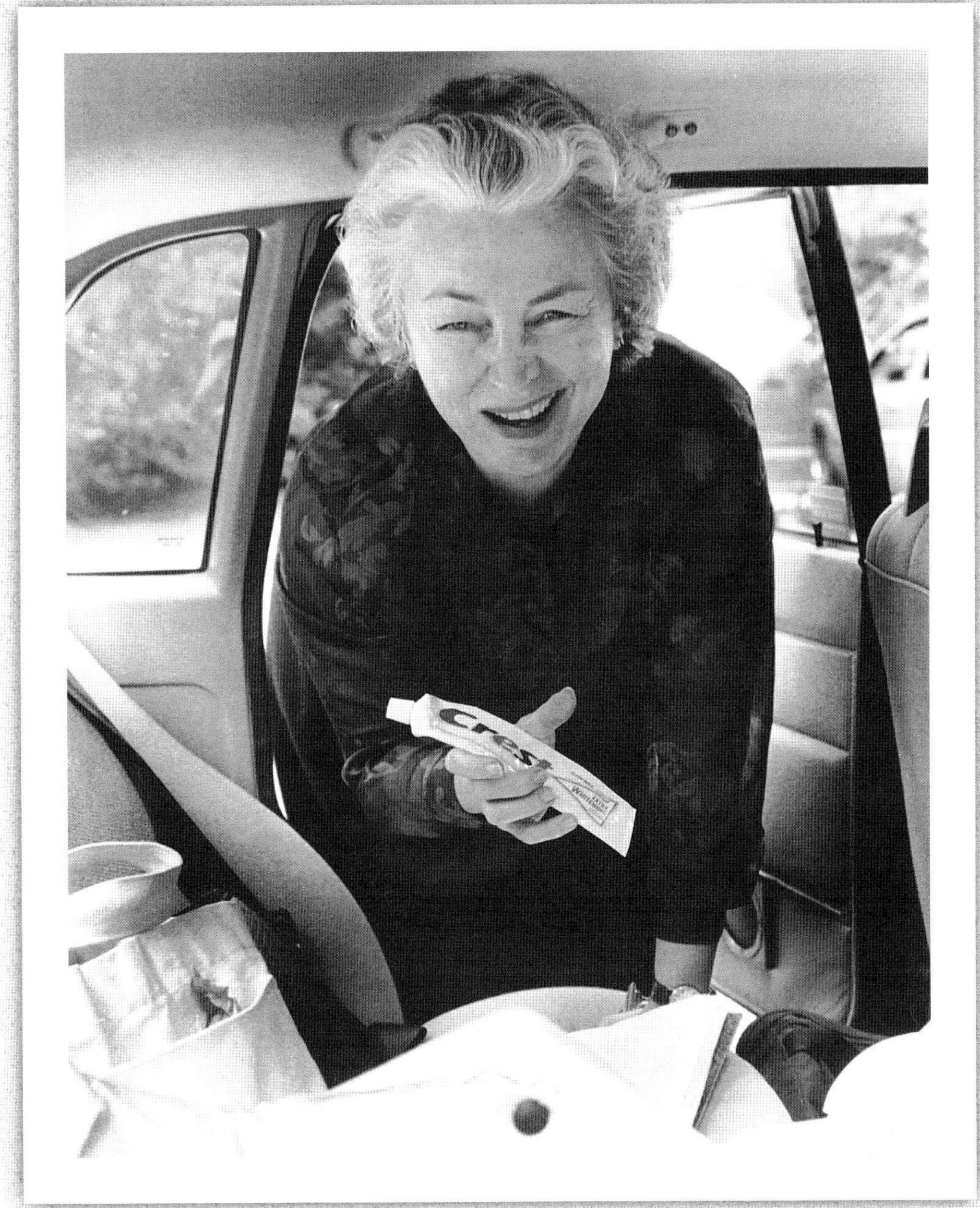
Crest

Monica McNeal
Television Reporter and Weekend Meteorologist

Communications Purse

My "Star Trek" cell phone is attached to the outside of my purse; inside are lots of itty-bitty compartments for my dozens of pens; my Splenda and Equal; and my "IFB," the television earpiece I wear to communicate with the station when I'm doing live shots.

I keep my makeup in a whole separate bag MUCH bigger than this purse!

Clouds have always fascinated me—I love reporting on the weather. This job is a blast! My dream job would be Al Roker's—he's the meteorologist on the *Today* show with Katie Couric.

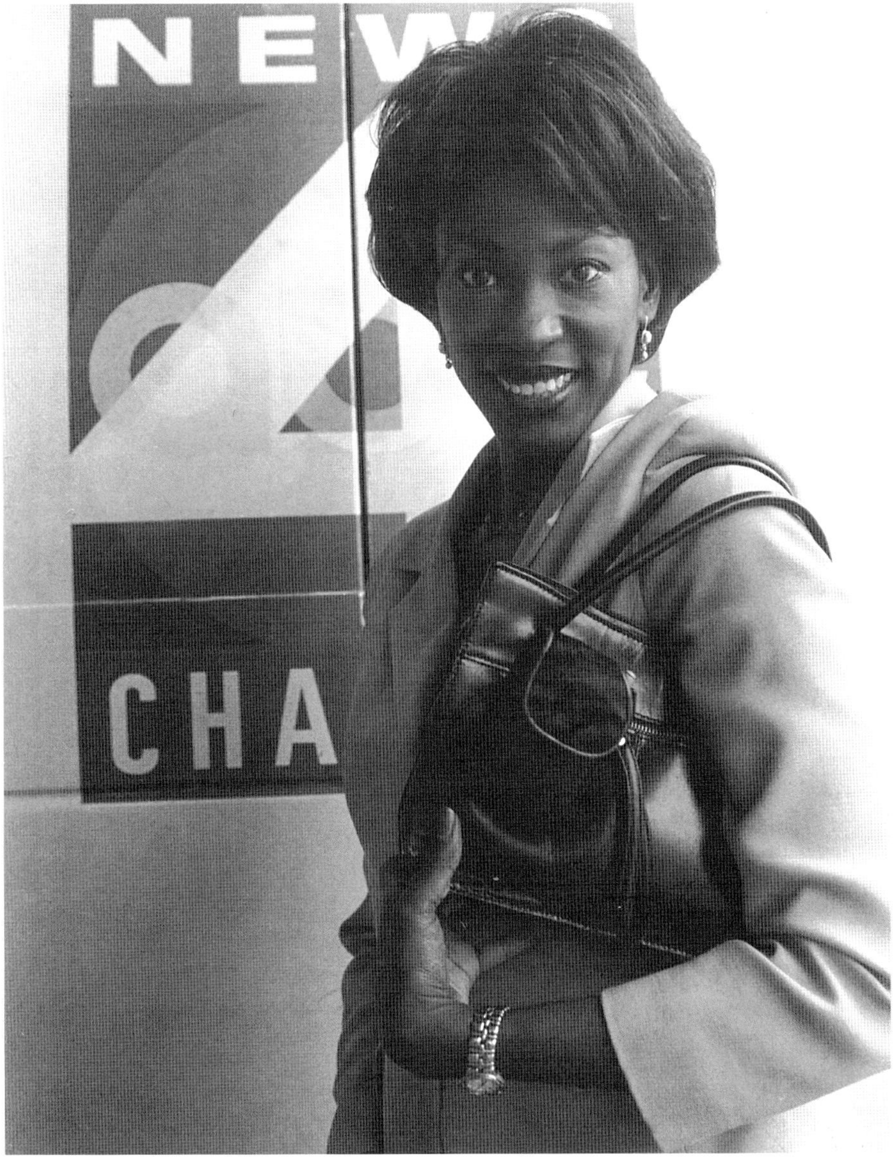
NEW
CHA

B.J. Kelly

Office Manager, Owner of Blooming Widow Enterprises

Santa Claus Purse

When I saw this purse at a Merle Norman Studio one June eight years ago, I said, “I HAVE to have it. It’s a little pricey, so I’ll put it on layaway and have it paid for by Christmas party time.”

I’ve carried it throughout the holidays ever since. When it’s not in use as a purse, it doubles as a Christmas ornament. I like to put it on the cedar chest at the foot of my bed.

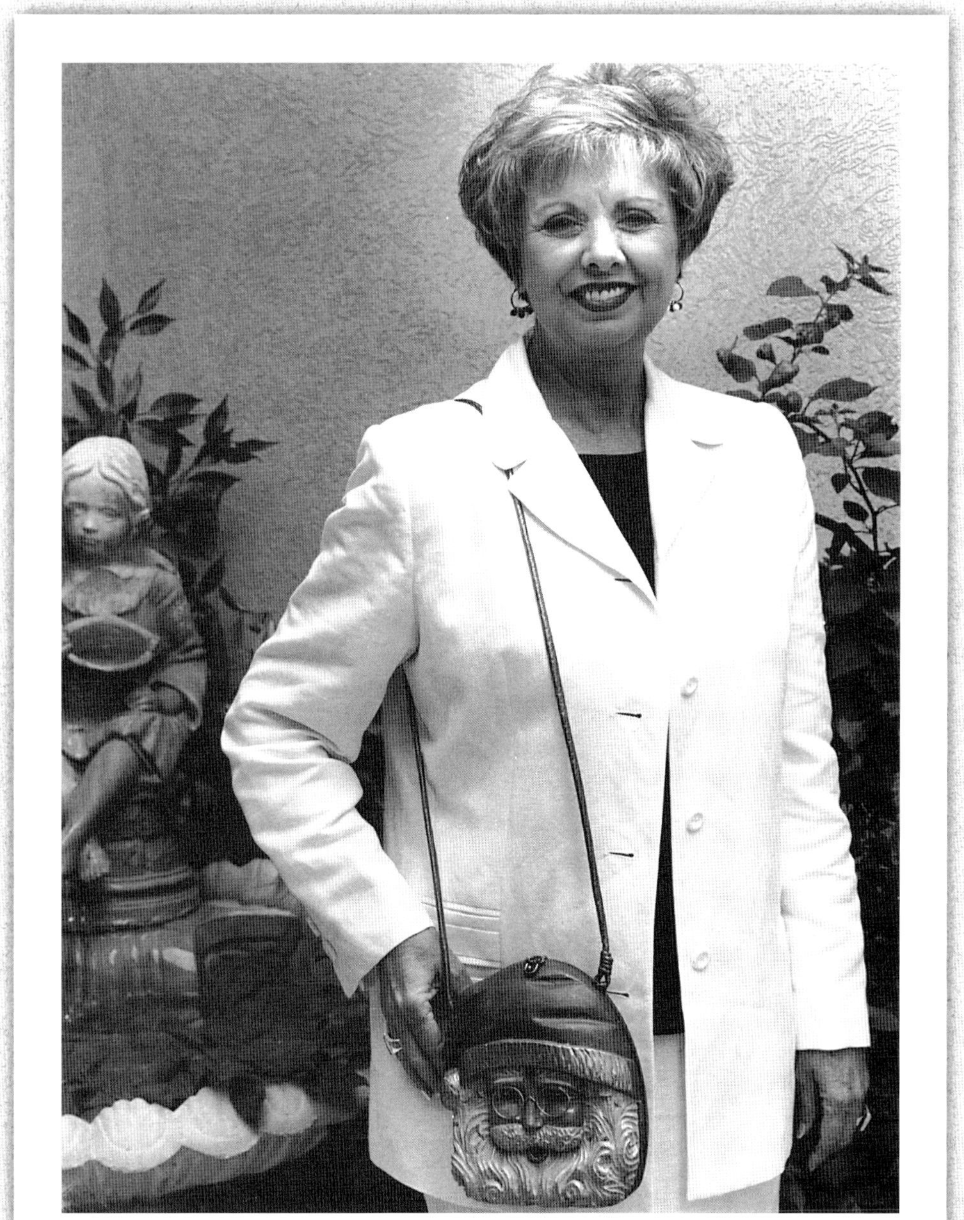

Gervais Hagerty
Student

Leopard Purse

I look for character in a purse,
not necessarily for practicality.
I don't need to carry much,
just keys, ID, and gum.
How did I choose this purse?
I didn't.
It chose me.

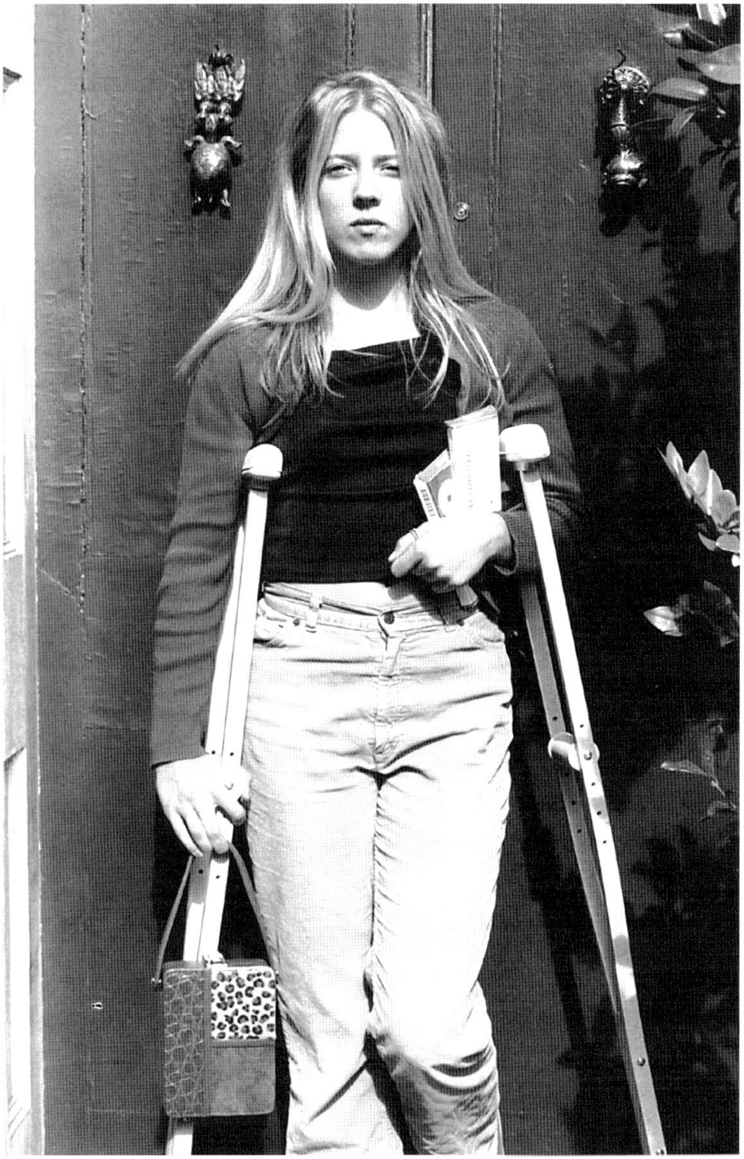

Madeline LaBoone

Banker

Paint Can with Peacock Feathers

I made this "Mad Bag" by gluing peacock feathers onto a new one-gallon Sherwin-Williams paint can. I have to be a serious person eight hours a day. When I go on lunch break or leave work, carrying this bag helps me be Madeline again.

You won't see another banker with one.

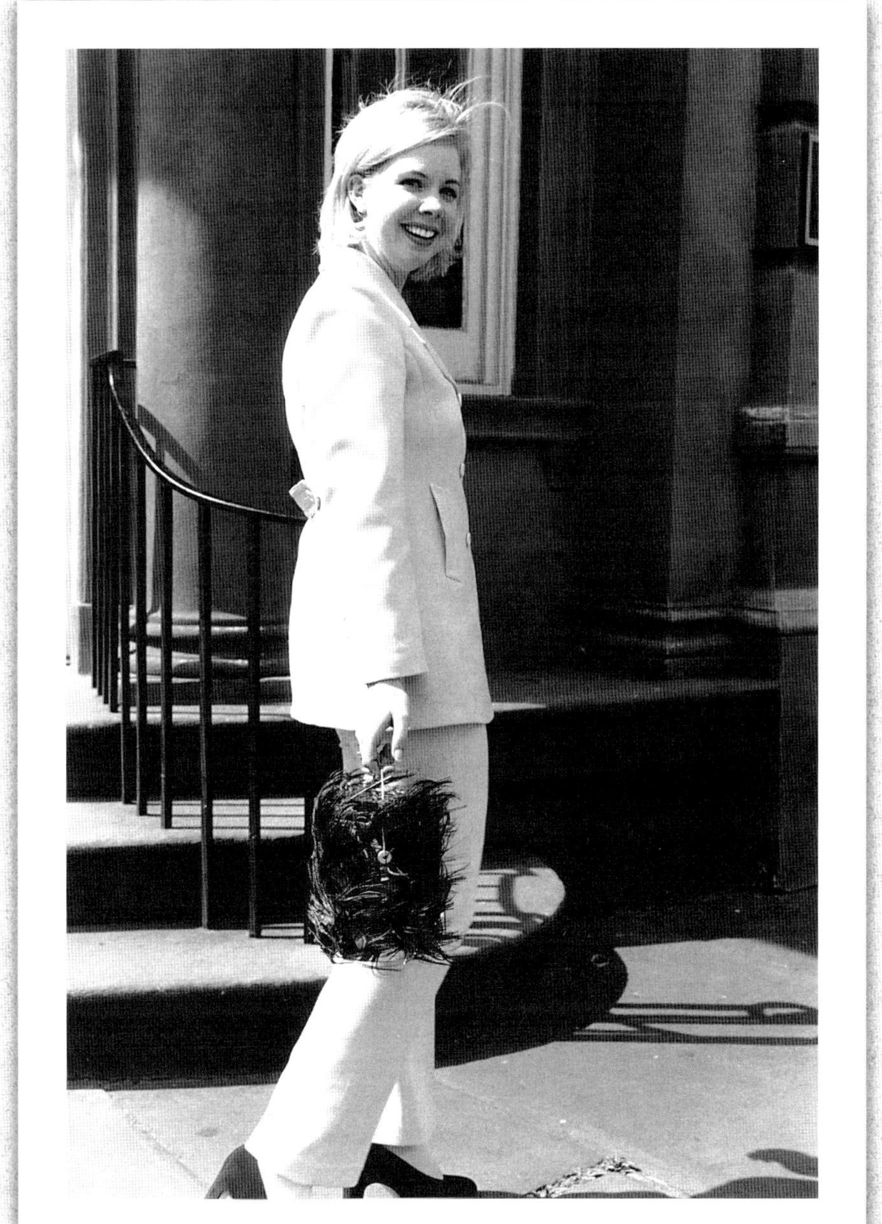

Khaki Wieters, Cameron Stoll, and Danielle Ziff

Friends

Gas Mask Bag

My purse is an authentic gas mask case that I found at an Army-Navy store. It's soft and has a half-moon shape. It buttons on the outside, and inside there are compartments that probably held knives or survival equipment.

I use it for everything except formals.

—Cameron Stoll *(center)*

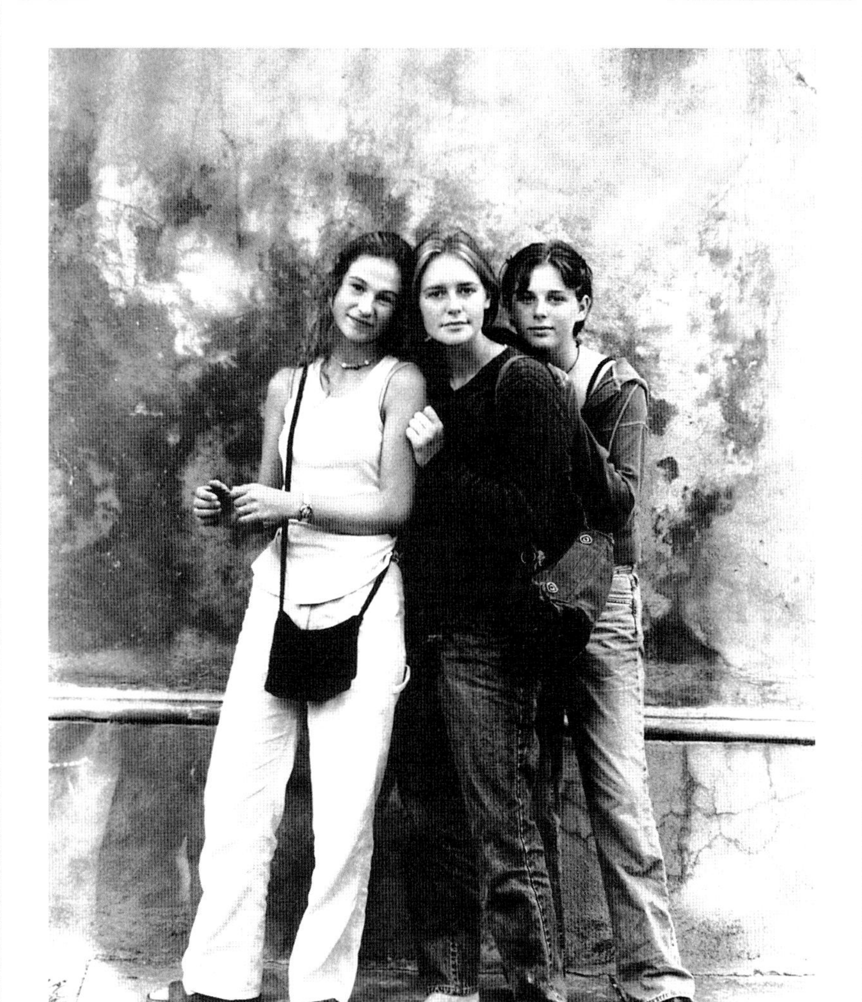

Bedell Broughton
Great-Grandmother

Carryall Purse

I carry all kinds of junk:
Candy, aspirin, a piece of cake.
Hat, ear bobs, and lye soap from the Piggly Wiggly.
Epsom salt to cool down when it gets too hot,
my lunch, a hairpin, and extra plastic bags
in case somebody on the bus has a package
that has broken down or come loose.

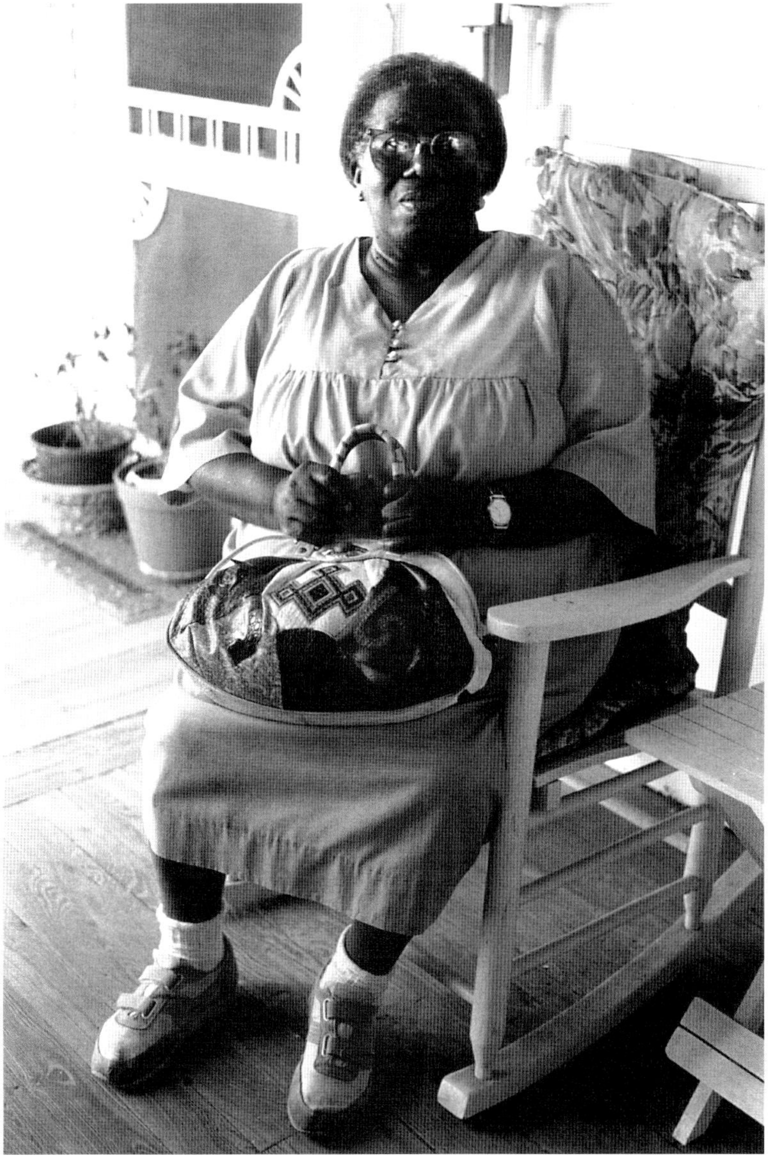

Antonia Paul Jackson
Artist, Sculptor, Videographer

Little Man Purse

I'm an admirer of and aspirer to Leonardo da Vinci and Thomas Jefferson, because everyone should be able to do everything, and everything cross-pollinates.

I bought this Little Man purse in New York City twenty years ago because of his toes—they're such a nice shade of watermelon. I wear him to parties—over a plain dress, usually. Inside I keep lipstick, Kleenex, and now glasses. Because I don't drink, he helps me have a good time at a party. He's my non-drinking partner.

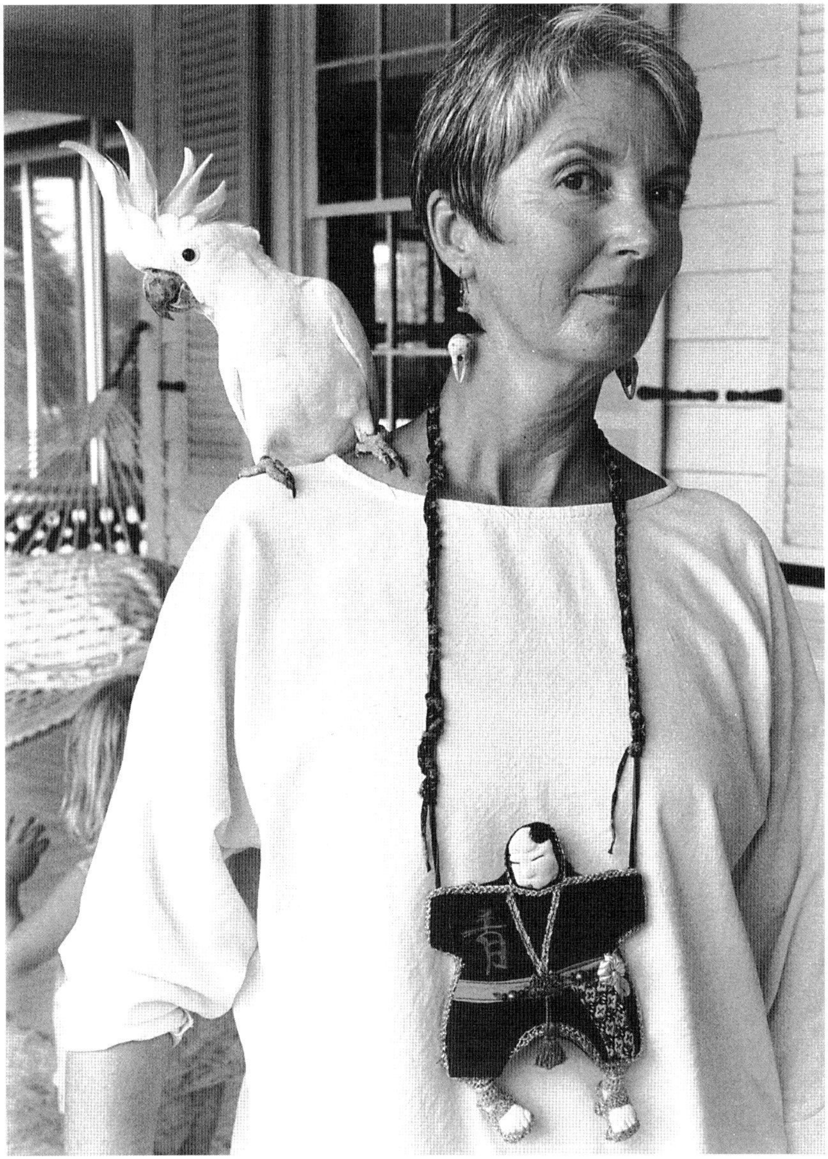

Laura and Marissa Jacobson

Sisters

Matriarchy Purses

These evening bags belonged to our great-grandmother, Mary Carello Klein. Her parents emigrated from Sicily to New York City, where they ran a fish store. By her twenties, she had risen above her immigrant status. She and her husband had money during the Depression and loved to travel. Some of these purses were bought in Paris.

My sister and I like to carry these purses to formals and proms. Anyone can buy a vintage purse; ours hold not only our family history but also a kind of power. They've been places, met people. This is their re-voyage. I want to retrieve the fantasy. Carrying one of these purses transfers, in a sense, my great-grandmother's power to me—the power to be more feminine, more confident, more beautiful. She was a role model for strength, confidence, knowing who you are. My goal is to be the same strong matriarch in the family I create.

—Marissa Jacobson *(right)*

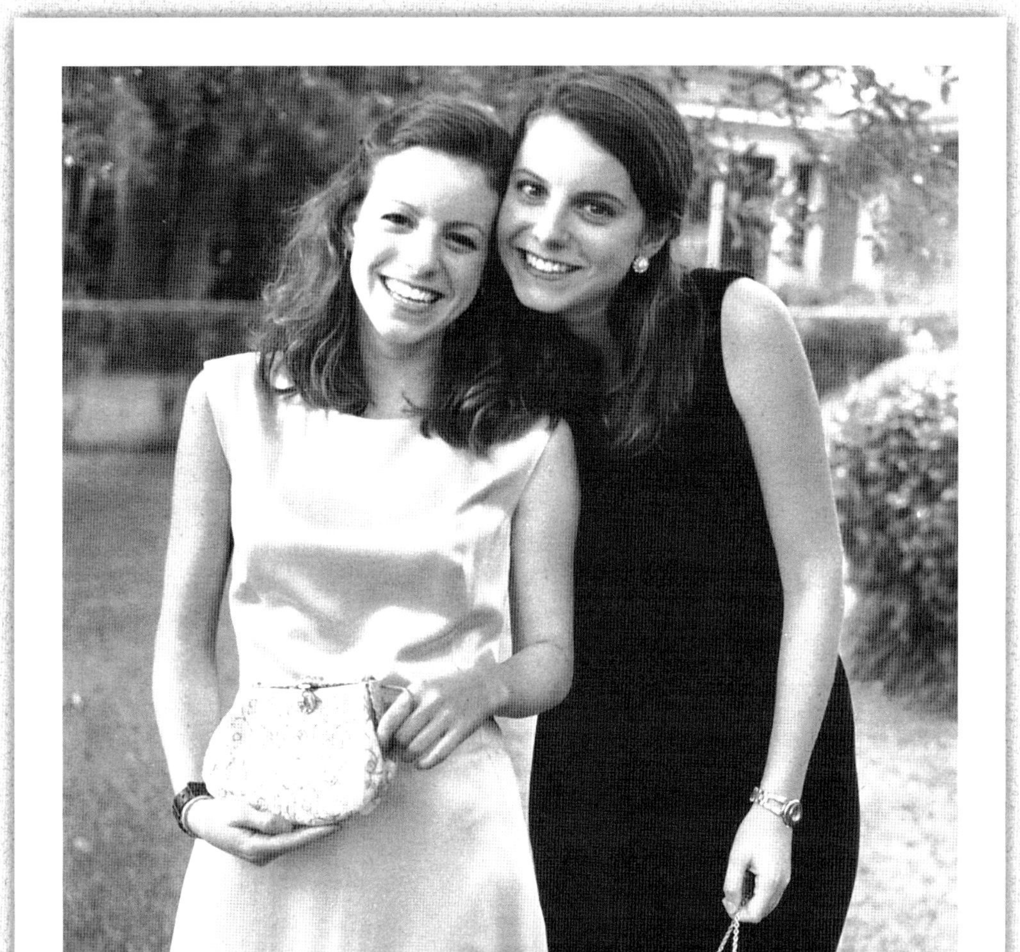

Molly Bradley Jackson

Iconoclast

Chicken Purse

I'm a boring Midwesterner from Illinois. An Army brat.

I got Chicken in 1993 from a children's shop in Soho. Why did I buy him? How could you not buy him? Look at the legs! The legs are squeezable! It sort of has knees. There's nothing better than chicken knees.

I'll tell you why I bought him. Because I hate it when people take their purses too seriously: "Look at me and my important Louis Vuitton or Gucci purse."

Once Chicken got left at a bar in Memphis. When we noticed he was gone, there was all-out panic. We drove furiously! Thank goodness Chicken was still there.

Last time I wore him was to a baby shower, to contrast with all the ladies in pearls and lace.

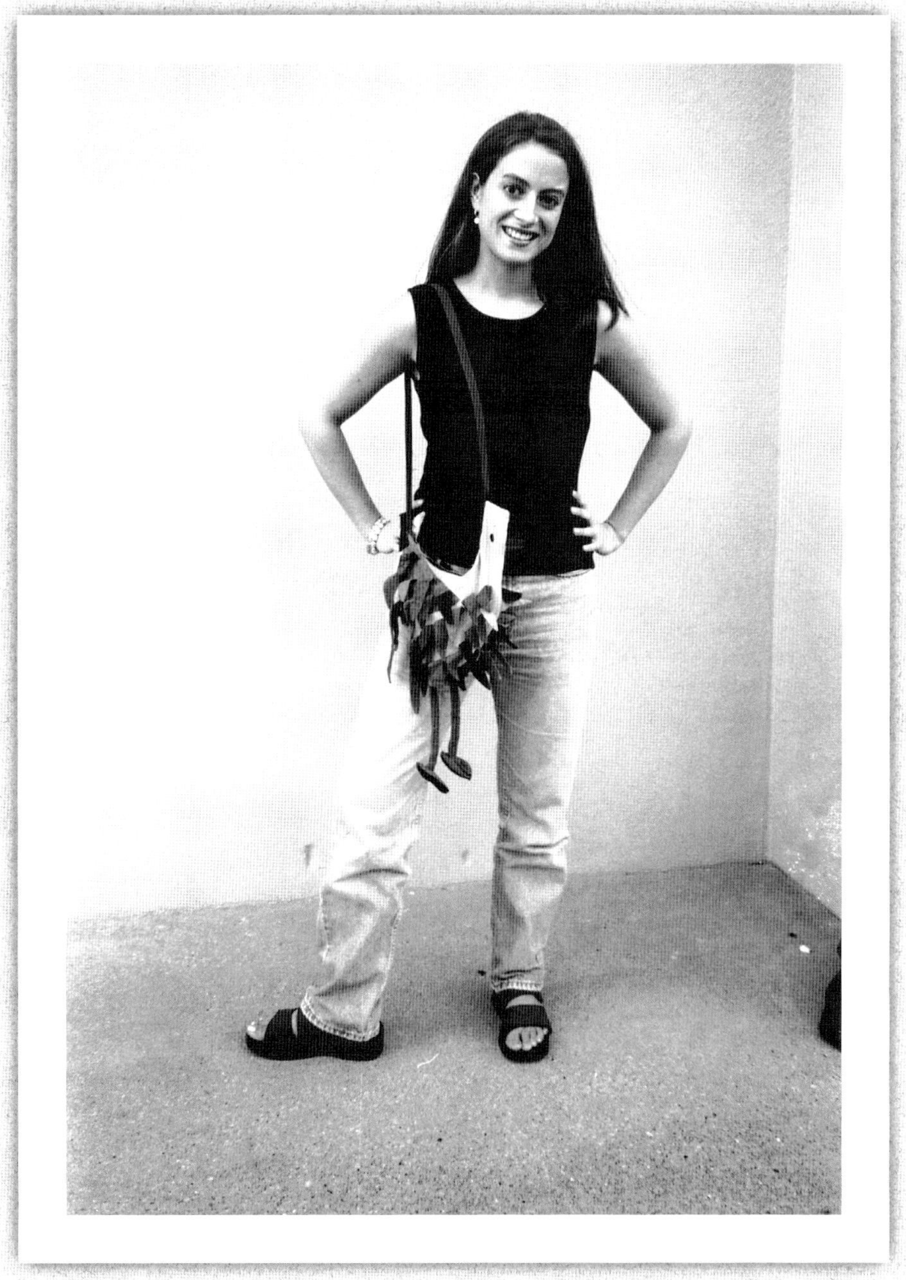

Harriet Smartt
Sentimentalist

Great Aunt Tee's Purse

This bag belonged to my Great Aunt Tee (Catherine McNeese), who lived in a hotel in my hometown of Tullahoma, Tennessee. She had been married to a roué who squandered her fortune. She was divorced and was as much a feminist and free spirit as a woman could be at that time.

Great Aunt Tee was like a character out of a novel. I loved to visit her in the hotel. She'd let me play dress-up with her clothes and bags. When she died, she left this evening bag and another to me.

This one is gold- and silver-beaded with fringe and a blue polka dot lining. I take it out when I dress up. I keep several things inside: a special mirror from my daughter-in-law; a key chain from my daughter, engraved with my nickname, Hattie; and an old linen-and-lace hanky.

I will leave one of them to my daughter and one to my daughter-in-law.

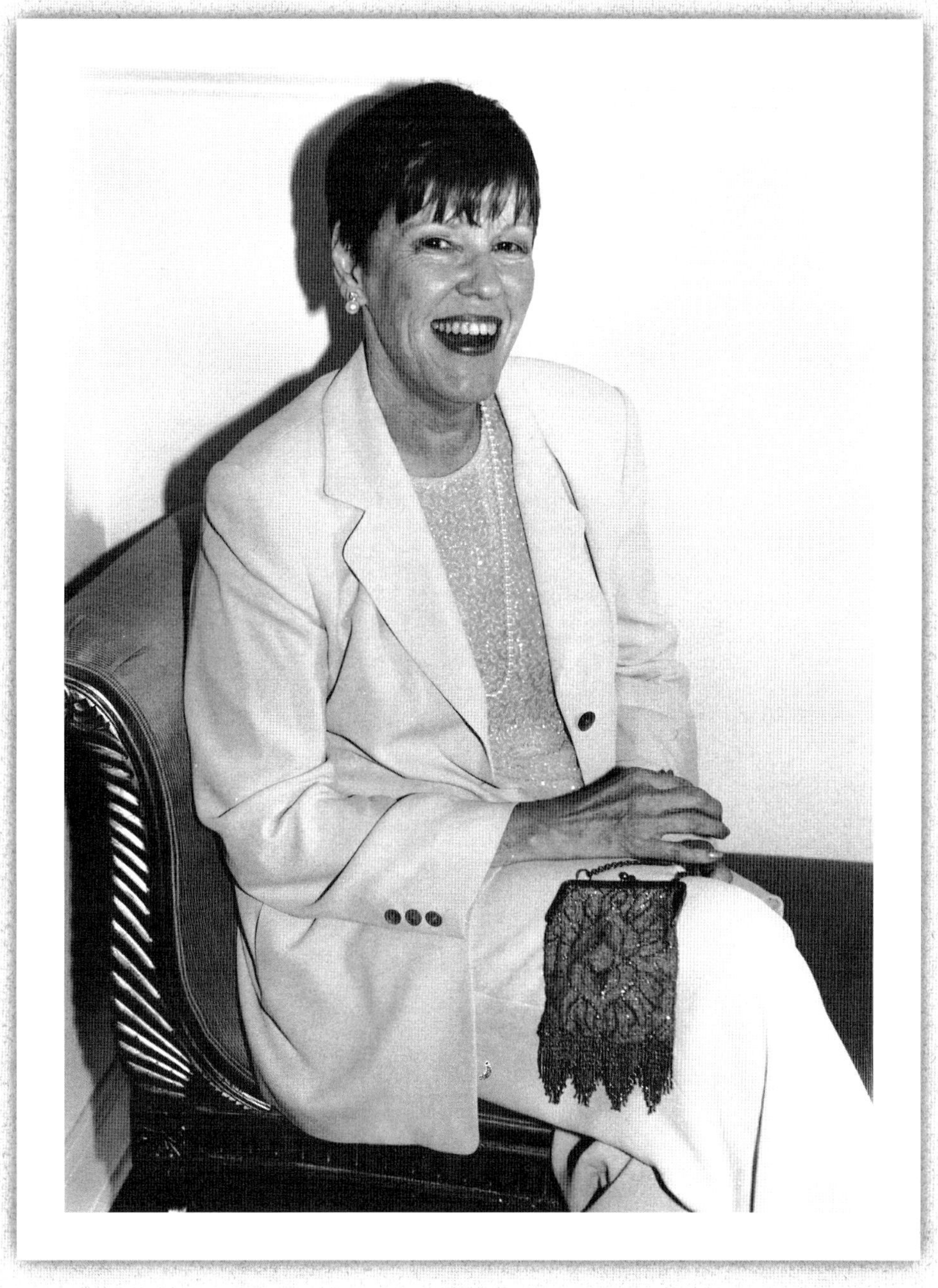

Eduardo Lemos

Purse Lover

Artist's Bag

Q: Will you tell me about your purse?

A: It is from the Chiapas region of Mexico.

Q: What do you keep inside?

A: Watercolors, drawing pencils, brushes, a special glue, brown drawing paper, medicines, my passport, a cell phone...

Q: Do you keep your keys there?

A: Yes! The keys to my art.

Q: Do you always carry it with you?

A: This purse is like a lover to me. Yes, I need everything in it.

Q: So you need it every day?

A: Ah! I need it every moment.

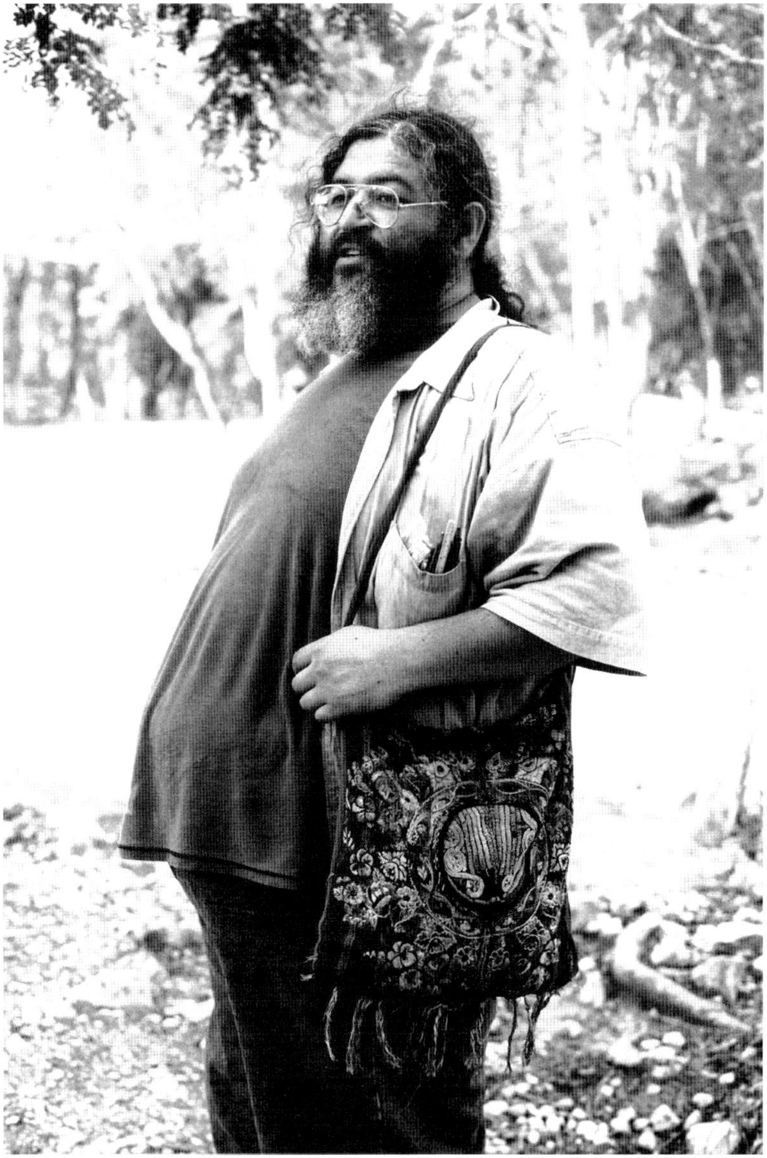

Jeannie Schroeder Lindler
Wife, Mother, Carpool Driver, Volunteer

Chinese Wedding Purse

On my sixth birthday, I received this purse as a present from an elderly spinster who had introduced my parents to each other. It came with a note that said, "For you to carry on your wedding day." The card, which I had until recently, was signed, "Love, Miss Elsie."

The purse sat in the cedar chest until my wedding day, March 20, 1976. I rode to the church with Daddy in a limousine that Barbara Walters had used two weeks before. I have two memories of that limo ride. One is pulling off my garter (which would have shown through my dress's fabric) and putting it in the Chinese wedding purse. My other memory is of dying for a ham sandwich, because I hadn't eaten all day.

Every time I use it—for weddings and important parties—it gives a warm memory of my wedding as well as of my childhood, when using the purse was something to dream about and look forward to.

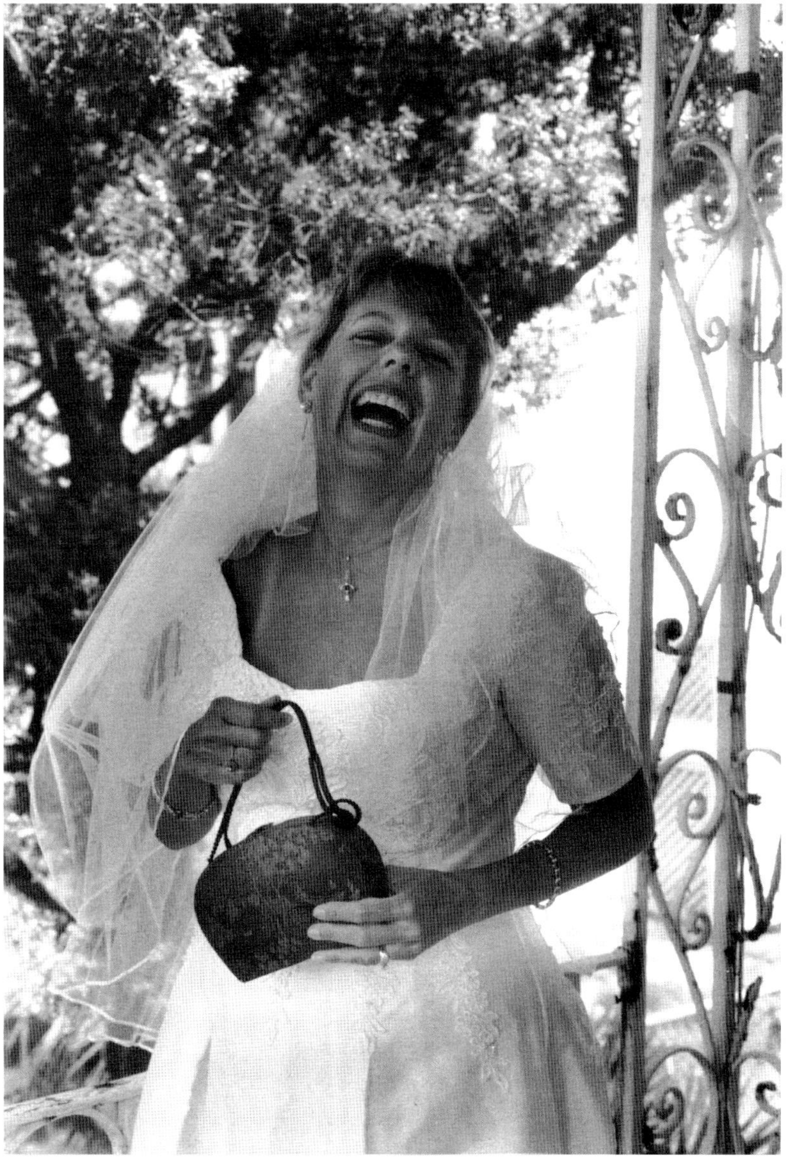

Vanessa Turner-Maybank
Tourism and Public Relations Specialist

Summer Purse

This light cream-colored purse was a gift from my significant other, Stanley, who's a teacher and a coach. I liked it so much—it fit my needs so well—that I bought another just like it in black. Now, except for church and special occasions, I change purses only twice a year. I'll switch over to the black version in the fall—my mother always said not to wear white after Labor Day!

As a working mom and caretaker of an elderly parent, I carry a lot of heavy things in my purse, including medicine bottles and several sets of keys. Stanley dropped by the office the other day and happened to pick the purse up. "What DO you keep in here?" he said. "You could use this as a substitute for lifting weights!"

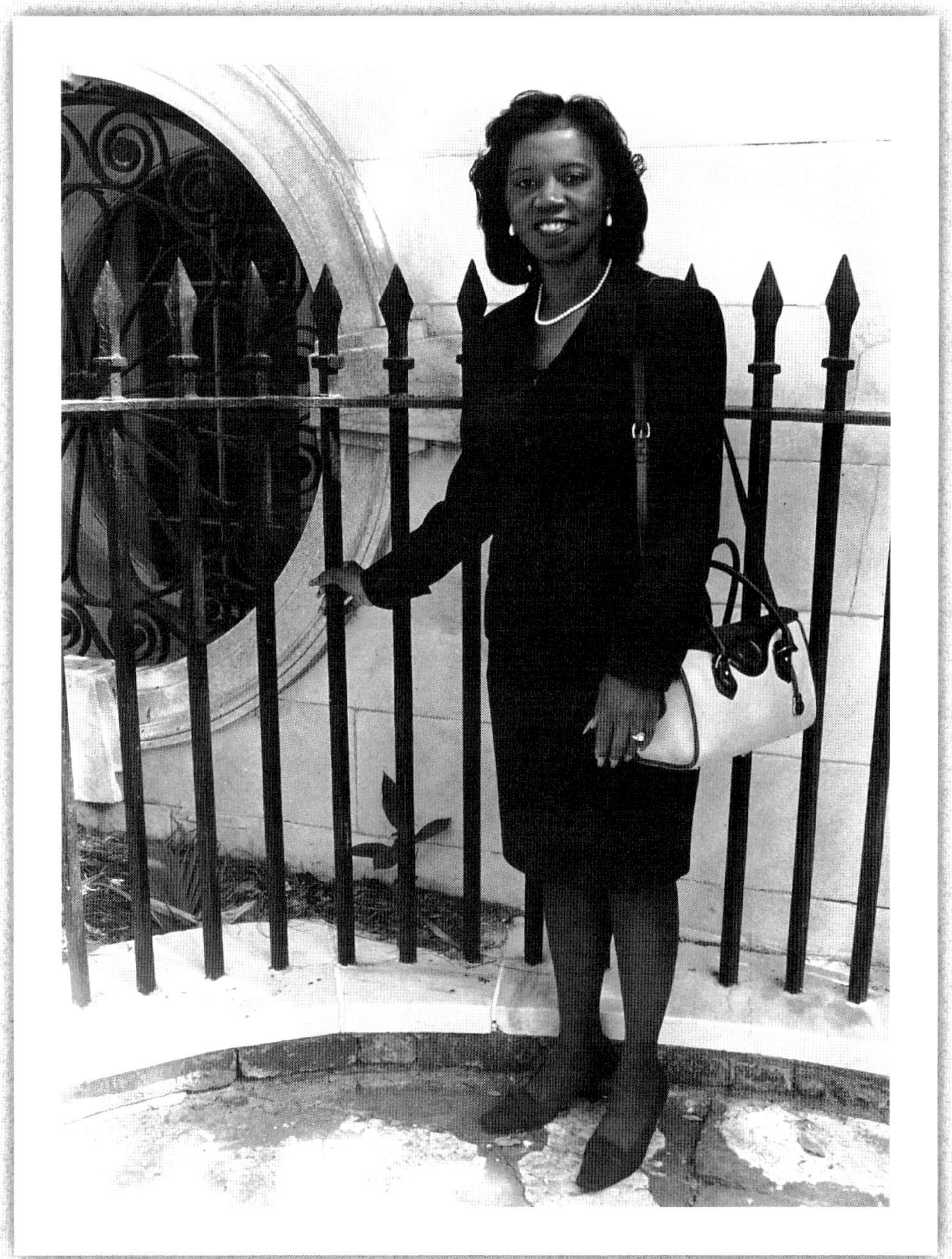

Cindy Smith
Halfway House Counselor

Lesser-of-Two-Evils Purse

It's not that I like or don't like purses. I just think they're necessary. I carry mine till it gets nasty and raunchy, usually two or three years. Then I stash it somewhere and buy another. When shopping, I'm not all that particular. I'll settle for the lesser of two evils.

It needs to have room for my pen, comb, plastic rain hat, candy, credit card case, bottle of Tylenol, cigarettes, and lighter. Oh, and I don't like to bother with zippers and snaps. I just leave my purse open.

As for the purse dress, I saw it in a catalogue and I thought it was sooooooo cute. It appealed to me. I like things with shoes on 'em, too.

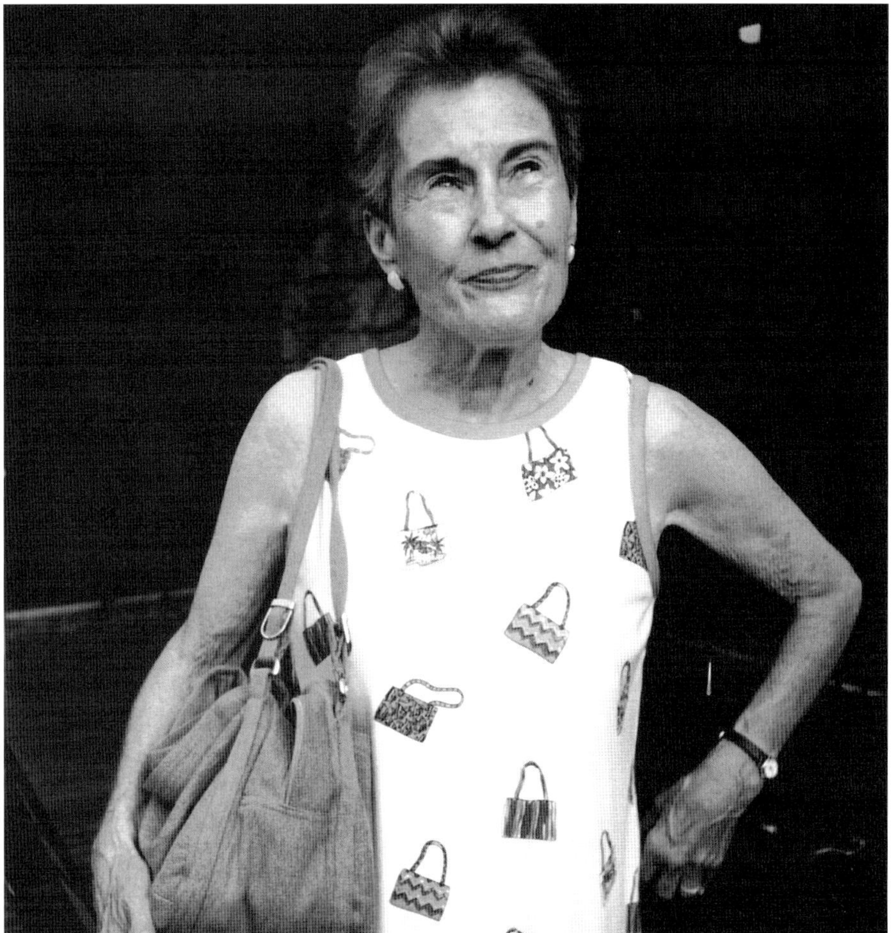

Karen Macke Weihs
Artist, Master Calligrapher, and author of *Out of My Mind*

Vase Purse

I bought this hand-painted leather vase purse at an art gallery in Highlands, North Carolina. It's signed "Janeyoo." I thought if I get tired of it, I can always use it as a vase. Being an artist gives you license to be a little crazy.

I like to wear the vase to art openings with carnations or roses inside it. "You're wearing your posies in your purse," people say.

Once I wore it to a dinner party, and the hostess put it on the table for the evening.

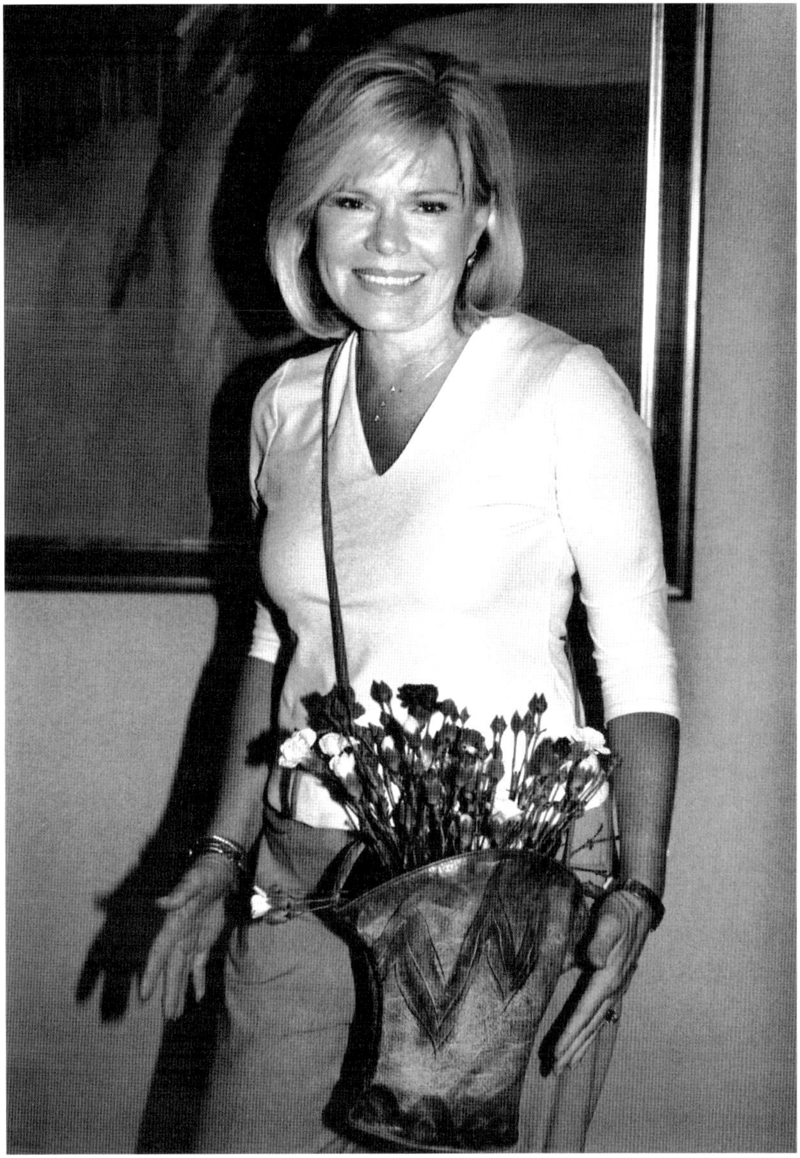

Jennifer Croker Poole
a.k.a. Splinkie
Website Maintenance Worker

Alien Being Bag

Once I worked in a conventional job at a real estate company, where I had to dress up every day. I sat in a cube. I hated it.

I love my work at Slicker, maintaining websites for rock groups like Jump, Little Children, SKWZBXX, and Blue Dogs.

I chose Splinkie for my e-mail address. The name just came to mind. Everyone asks, "Why Splinkie?" I have no answer for that.

I bought this bag at a store in London that's dark, neon, and loud. I spotted it out of a whole storeful of bizarre things. When I bought it, I had no idea how much it would become a part of me.

I take it everywhere I go. The bag is strapped over my shoulder with Velcro. I love the alien cartoon (not that I think I'm animated or cartoonish). It's futuristic, not scary or threatening. And it's not a Teletubby.

My roommate says I dress like a boy. The style right now is all the dainty, little girly bags. I could never have one because I couldn't fit anything in there.

If I'm going someplace dressed up, I have to think, "Oh, what do I do now?" I usually just shove my wallet and key in someone else's bag.

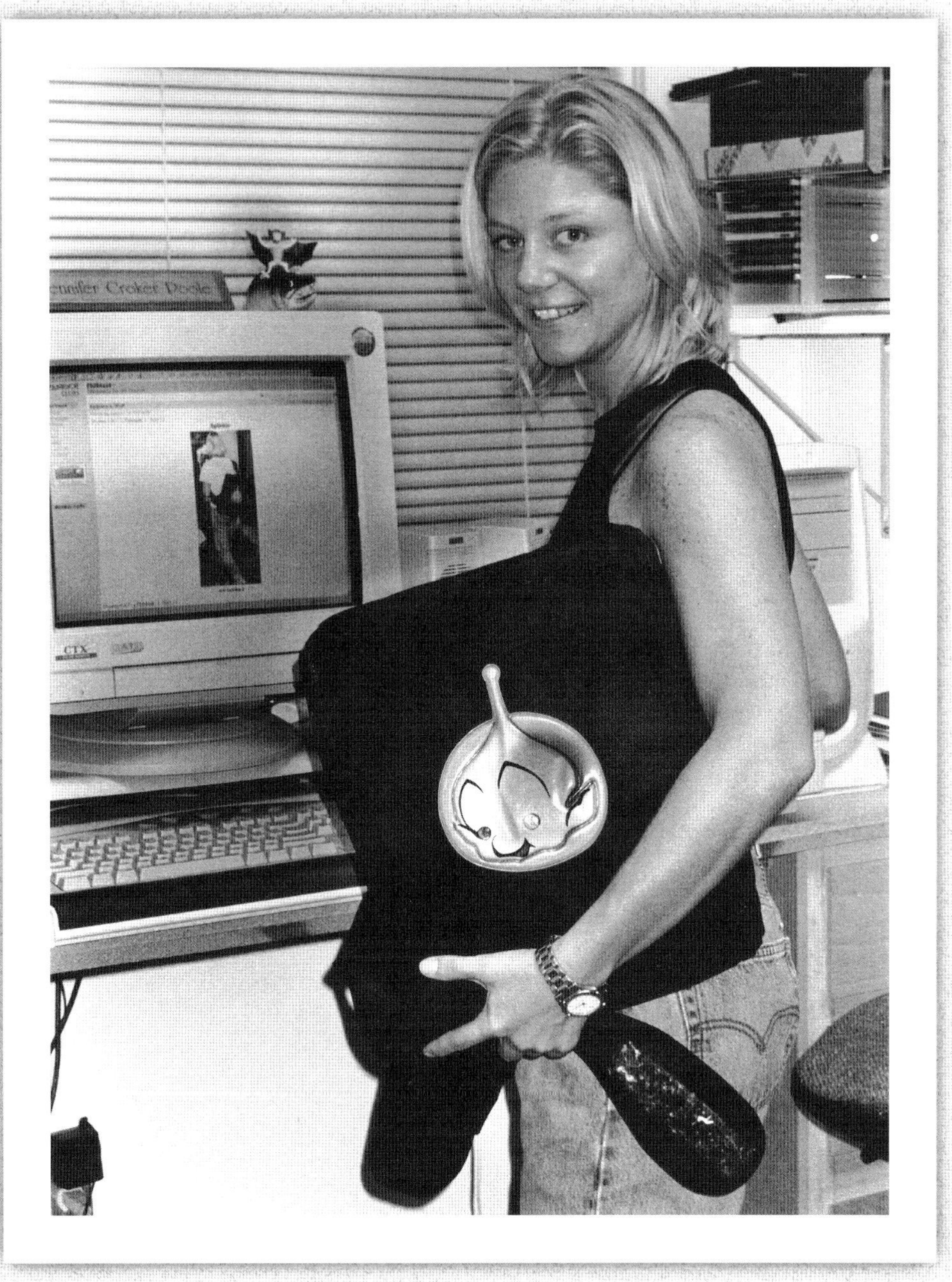
CTX

Carson and Curry
Best Friends

Teen Purses

Carson: Keys

Curry: Bus pass

Carson: Breath mints

Curry: Lip gloss

Carson: Pictures of my friends

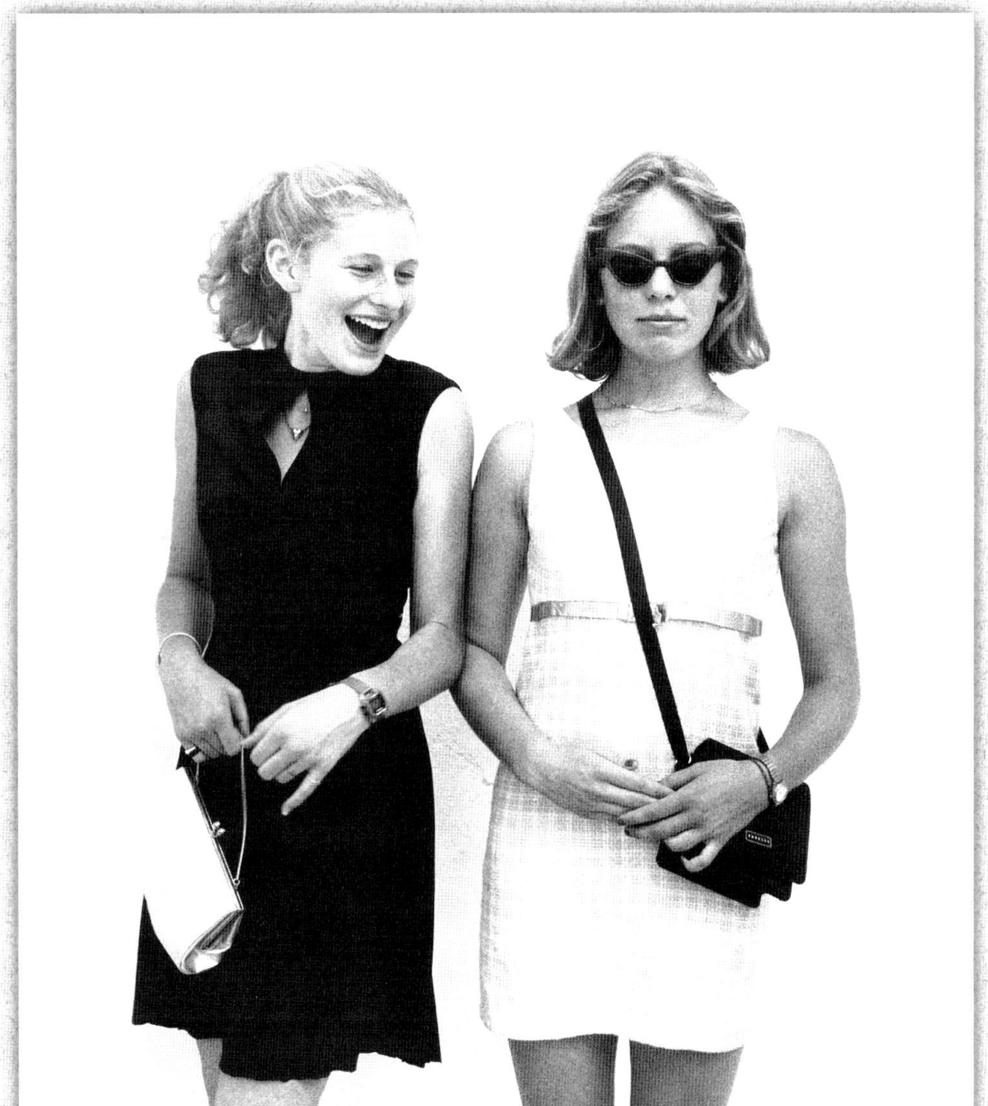

Enid Denise Jones Moreno

Nursing Assistant

Safety Purse

I like this purse because it's big enough to hold all my junk. I always have the things most people carry, plus deodorant, floss, cups, hair weaves, glue for the hair weaves, Sugar Babies, and Candy Drops. I'm ready for just about anything.

My purse is like my Volvo. I love a Volvo. It keeps going and going. It never breaks down. I can carry a lot in it. Everything's attached—no snaps, no zippers.

I feel safe in my Volvo. I feel safe with my purse.

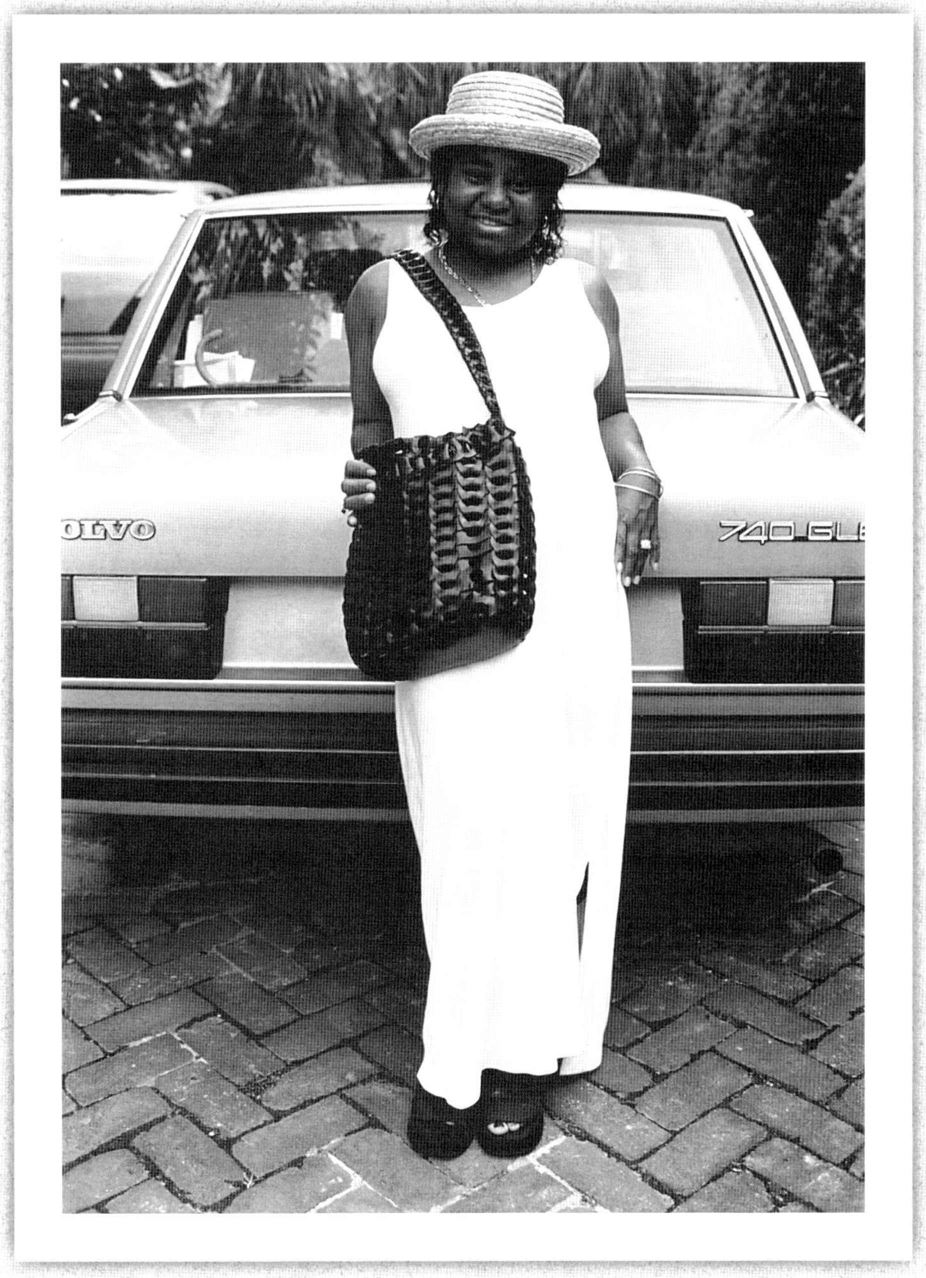
OLVO
740 GL

Jeri Cabot, Ph.D.

Professor, Feminist, Political Scientist

Purse of Hopes

I do see feminism as a cerebral movement that, first and foremost, is about changing ideas, world views, and attitudes. I don't view it so much as a street movement anymore. I see feminists all around us. They're carrying briefcases, backpacks, diaper bags, Italian purses. And that's what's so wonderful about the movement at this time: Feminists are everywhere. We are so far beyond the stereotype of being isolated or being disgruntled man haters. It's an empty definition.

I do keep my hopes in my purse and I am a very hopeful person. I imagine myself doing lots of interesting and diverse things in the future. I keep announcements of new books I want to read, workshops and conferences I want to attend, places I want to travel. I always hope that I'll actually order that book, attend that conference, and travel to that new destination.

I suspect that even though both men and women carry briefcases, women are more likely to take parts of the home with them. Traditionally, it has just been cosmetics; but now that women are in the workforce, it's likely to be things related to home life, such as remnants of children or books or travel plans, or a note about the PTA meeting.

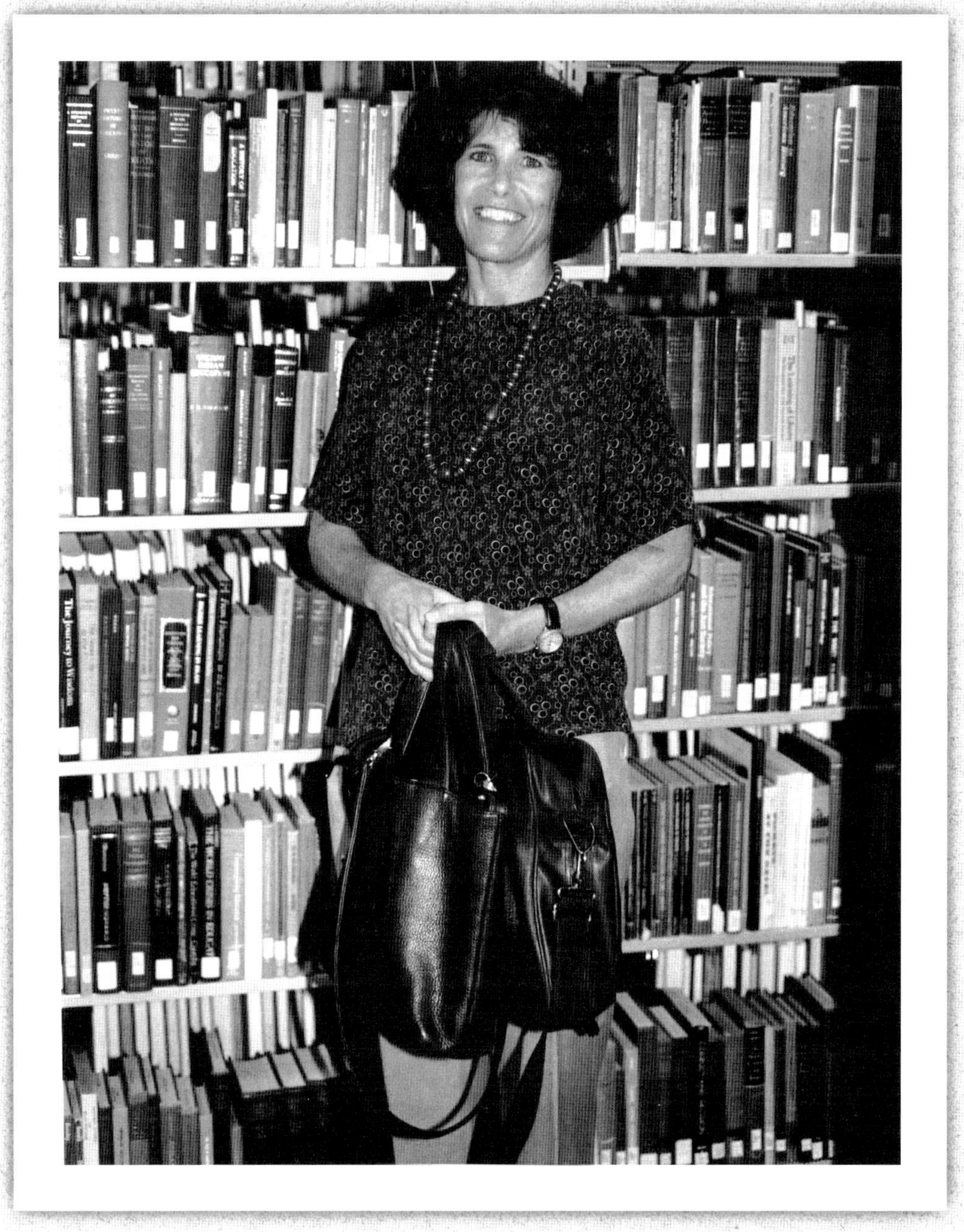

Mary Norton
Creator of Moo Roo Custom Handbags

Casual Pocketbook

After my two girls Micah (Moo) and Reilly (Roo) were born and I needed a part-time job, I had a dream. In the dream I was putting real flowers on a purse. The next morning I felt compelled to go buy silk flowers and attach them to evening bags. My first four sold in two days. Shortly after, an actress was pictured carrying one in *People* magazine. My success has happened that way, by a series of flukes.

My own pocketbook? I hardly ever dress up!

Here's the stuff I usually carry:

A bee sting kit

Baseball men Band-Aids

The glasses I never wear

Safety deposit box key

A list of places where I want to go shopping in Europe

A broken watch

Broken necklace

Scope

Cortaid

Checkbooks to three different accounts

A tampon

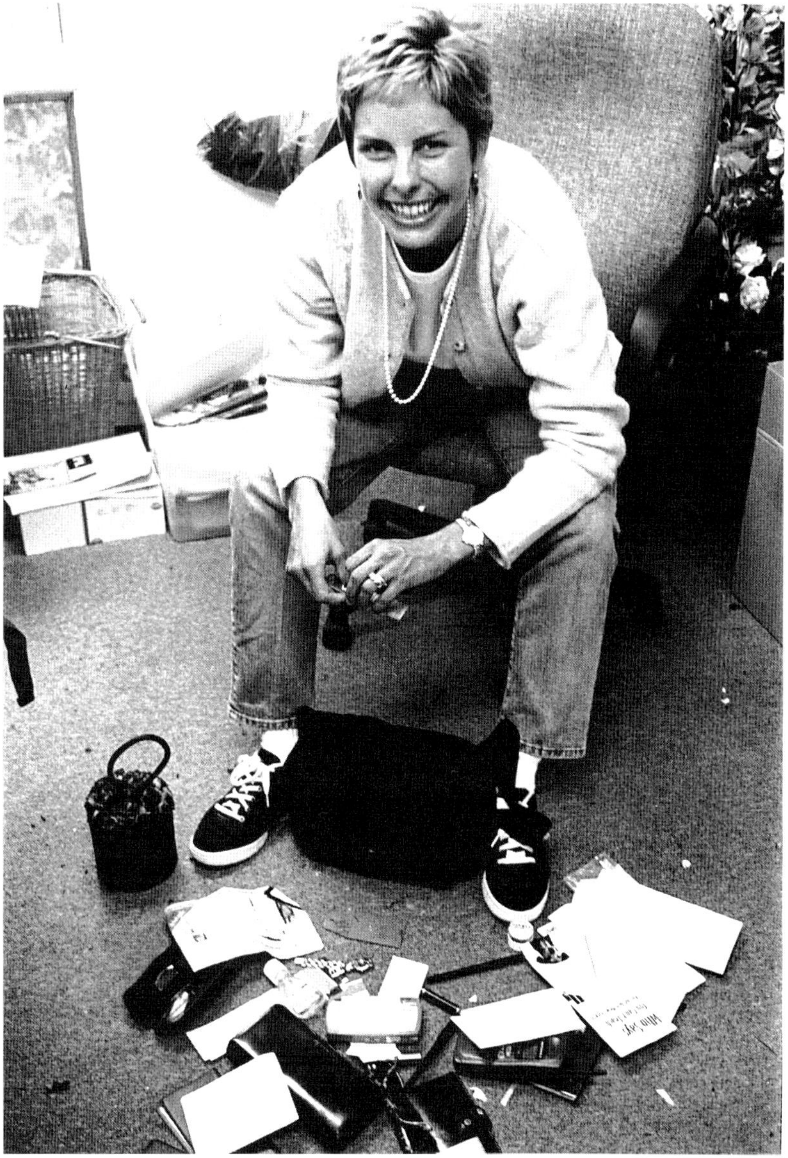

Brittany Alexandra Gudas
a.k.a. B.A.G.S.
Owner of Seventeen Original
Moo Roo Handbags

The Favorites

At first I didn't like my initials, because everyone made fun of me and called me "Bag Lady." My mom began collecting Moo Roos for me when I first drew the symbol. I added an "s" to my initials, because Gudas has an "s" in it. Now I use my initials all the time.

P.S. I never carry a purse. I think they're a *pain* to carry.

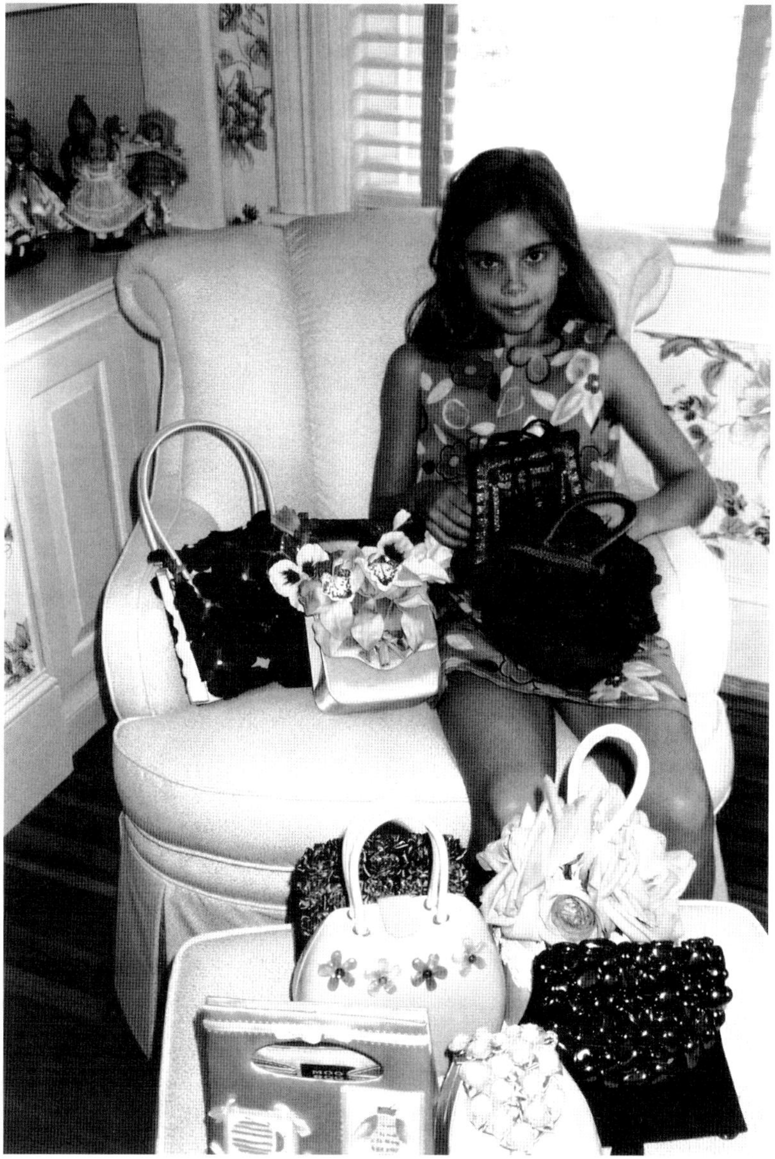

Rachel Fleury

Creative Writing Student

New Jersey Purse

I was born in New Jersey on February 7, 1986, and lived there until I was five. I went to Montessori School. When I was seven, we lived on a boat in the Bahamas, where I was home schooled. Every week I read at least one or two books. I like Gary Soto, Madeleine L'Engle, and Salman Rushdie. When I was little, I liked Shel Silverstein.

New Jersey is where I'm from, even though I don't live there anymore. I like the South but I miss the snow. New Jersey is my state.

A friend of Mom's gave her this patch, and she gave it to me. I had it for two years before deciding what to do with it. One night I sewed it onto blue fabric by hand, then attached a narrow, black grosgrain ribbon for the strap. It took about forty-five minutes.

When I wear it to school, the kids tease me and call me a Yankee, but I don't mind, because WE won.

I don't think the patch would have traveled all the way to me had it not been intended for me. It would have gone somewhere else—like the trash.

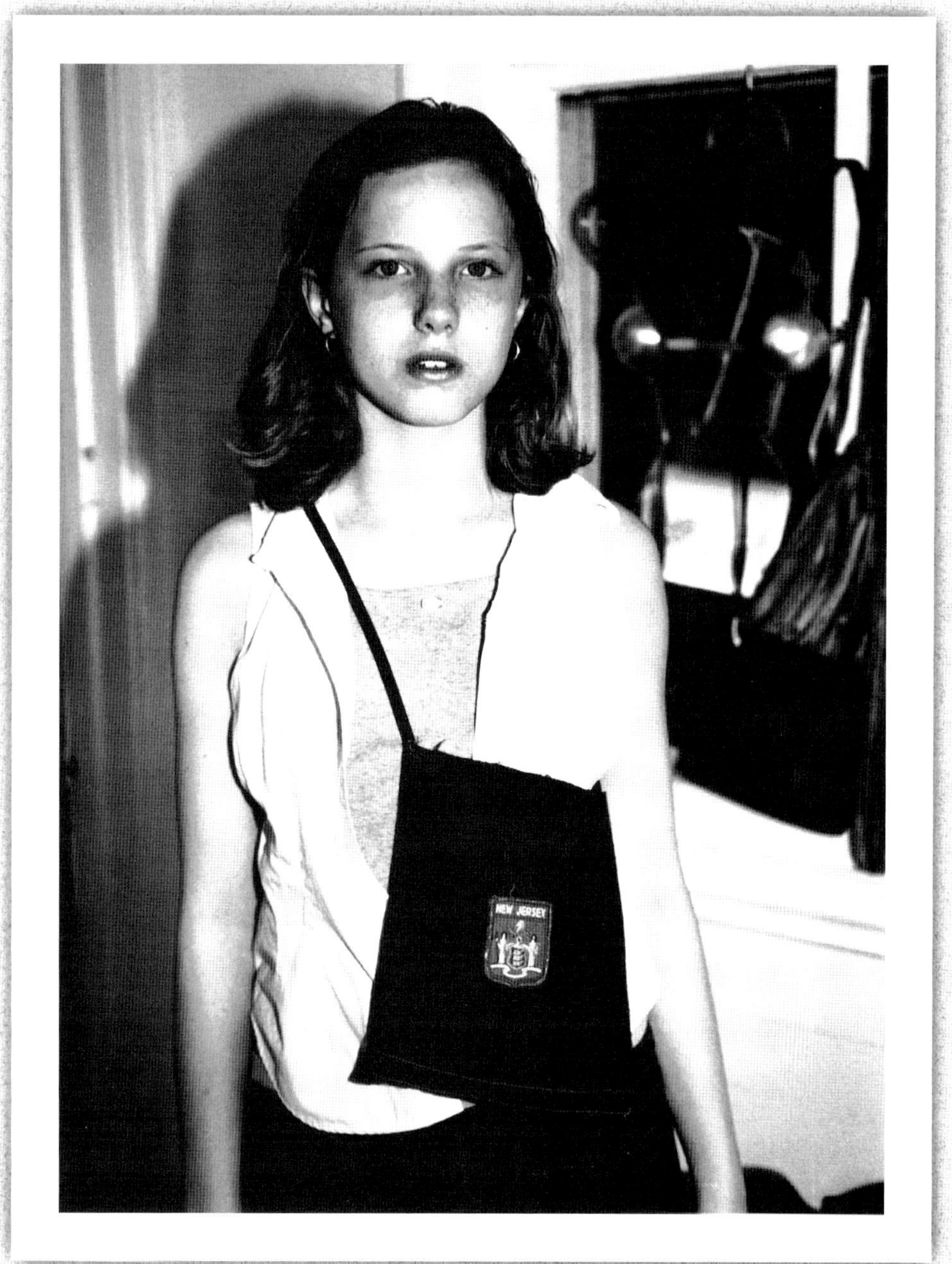
NEW JERSEY

Montye DuBose
Accessorizer

Harlequin Purse

As a girl coming off the farm and going away to school, I always thought a purse identified you, especially a smart-looking bag.

I've got to have a bag to match every pair of shoes. Actually, I always use two bags. One is for looks, and the other stays in the trunk of the car to hold all the real stuff—my inhaler, lipsticks, bank book, and business cards.

As a child I had German measles. By the time I graduated high school, I was legally blind. But that never stopped me from doing anything. I was thirty-two before I knew it was a big to-do to be partially sighted. I still cut my own hair and put on my own eye makeup. Oh, I could do that in the dark!

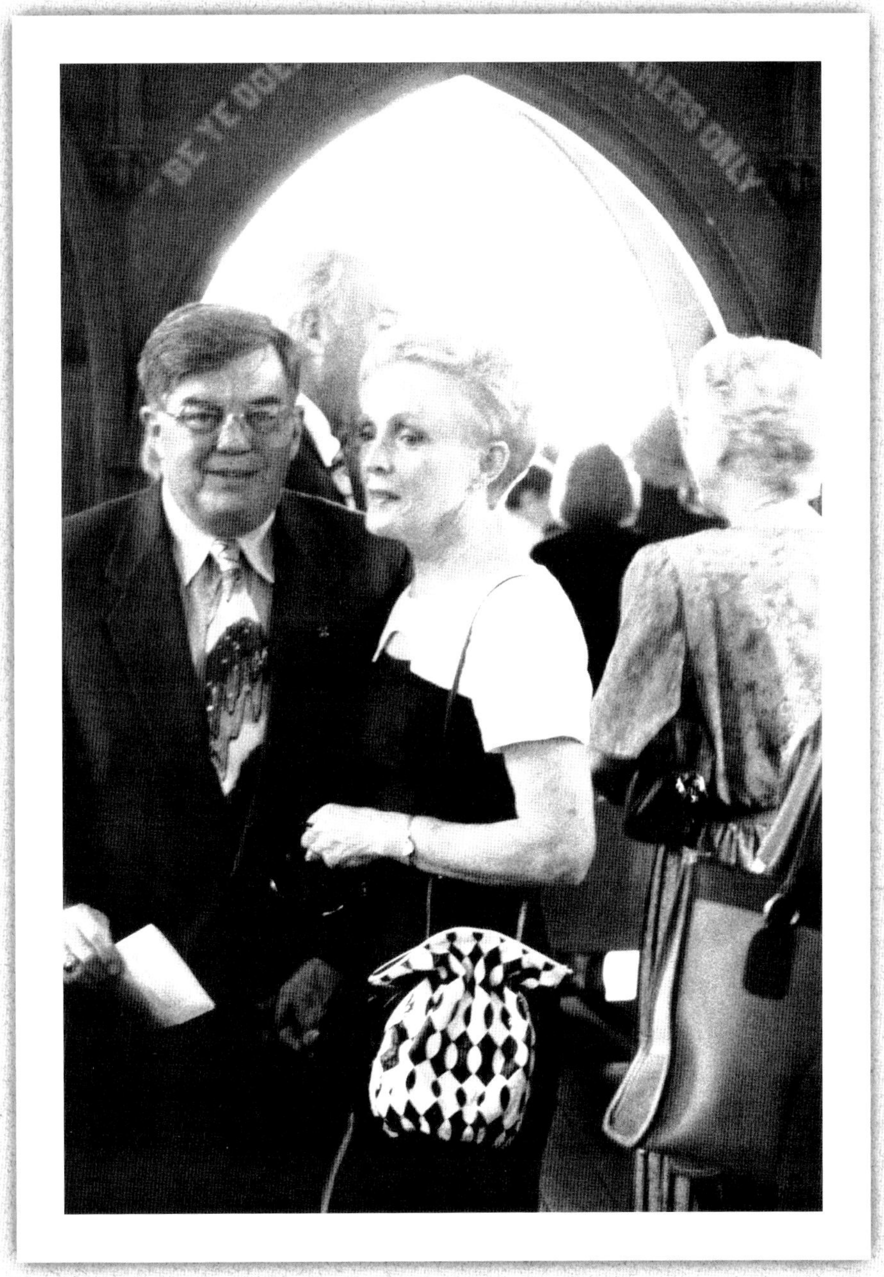

Corday Rice
Actress, Student

Bunny Purse

Dogs react to this purse in different ways.
Some bark, some bite,
some want to play.
My purse can get dirty.
I gave it a bath recently and blew it dry.

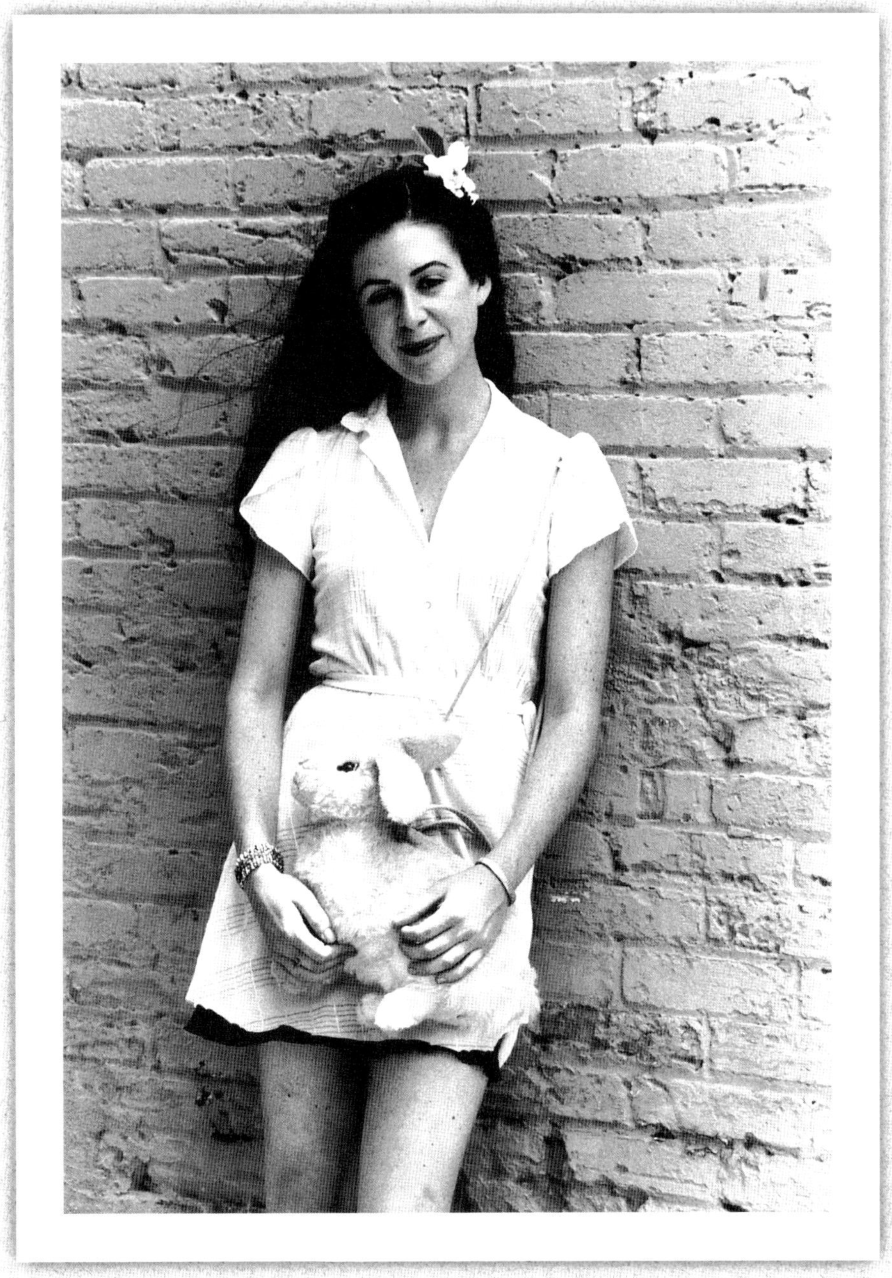

Priscilla Drayton
Operating Room Nurse

My Baby Purse

I call this purse "my baby" because we've been so close for so many years. It's genuine leather—broken-in, broken down, soft, and cuddly.

We've been through the wringer together, my purse and I, but I can't part with it even long enough to send it for repairs. This purse is my baby—I could never throw it out!

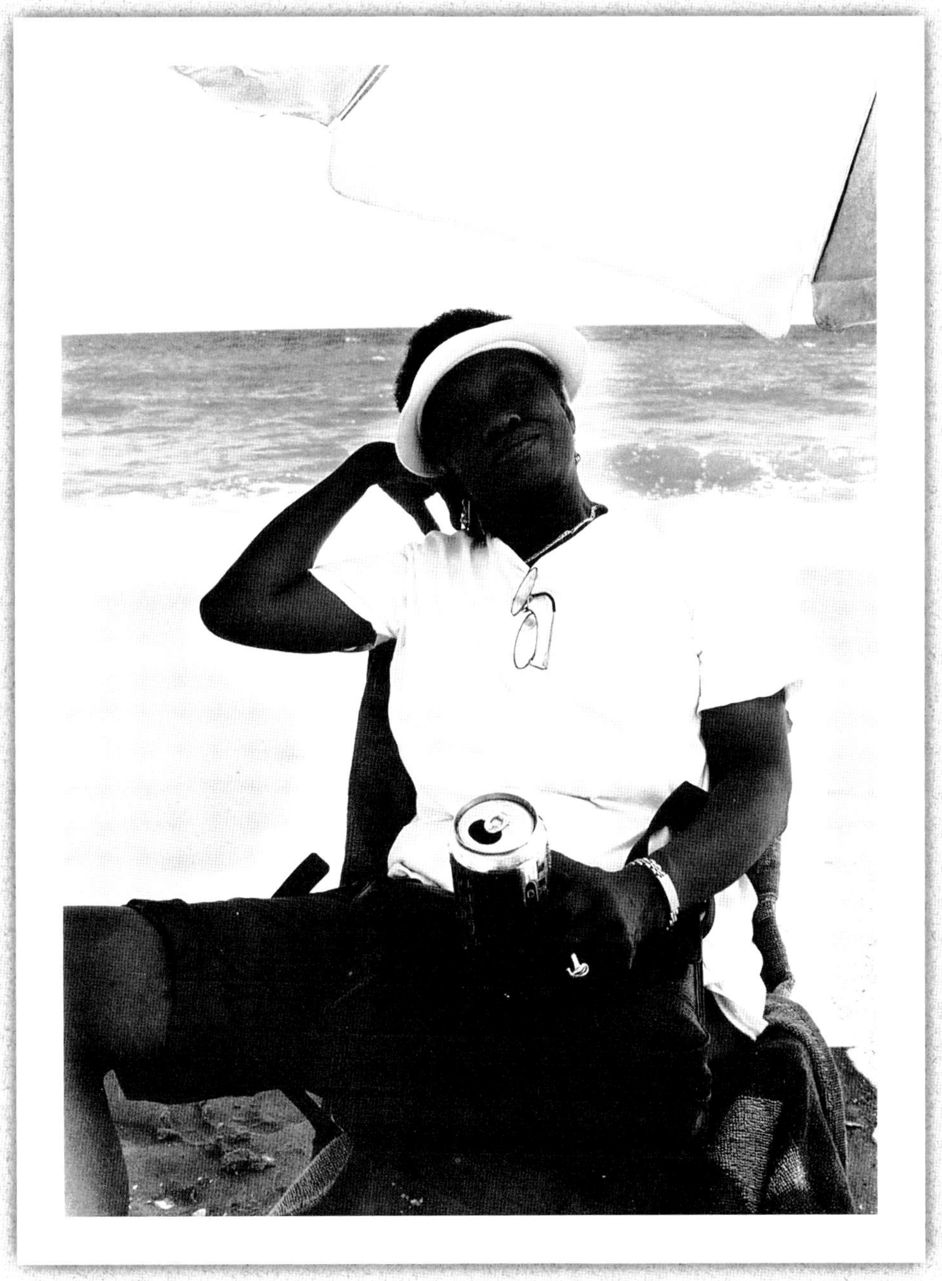

Jessie Kendall
Student

AIDS Awareness Purse

I'm an only child who was born in Raleigh, North Carolina, in 1979. My ambition is to be a graphic designer with an emphasis on social concerns. I have a problem with things being merely aesthetic without substance.

A friend in high school made this purse for me six years ago. On a trip to New York, I made a donation to help people with AIDS. Each donor was given a red ribbon, and I pinned mine on my purse, where it has remained for several years.

I felt that the least I could do, or anyone could do, was remember and recognize AIDS victims. They don't deserve to die. Everyone should do something to help, even if it is something small.

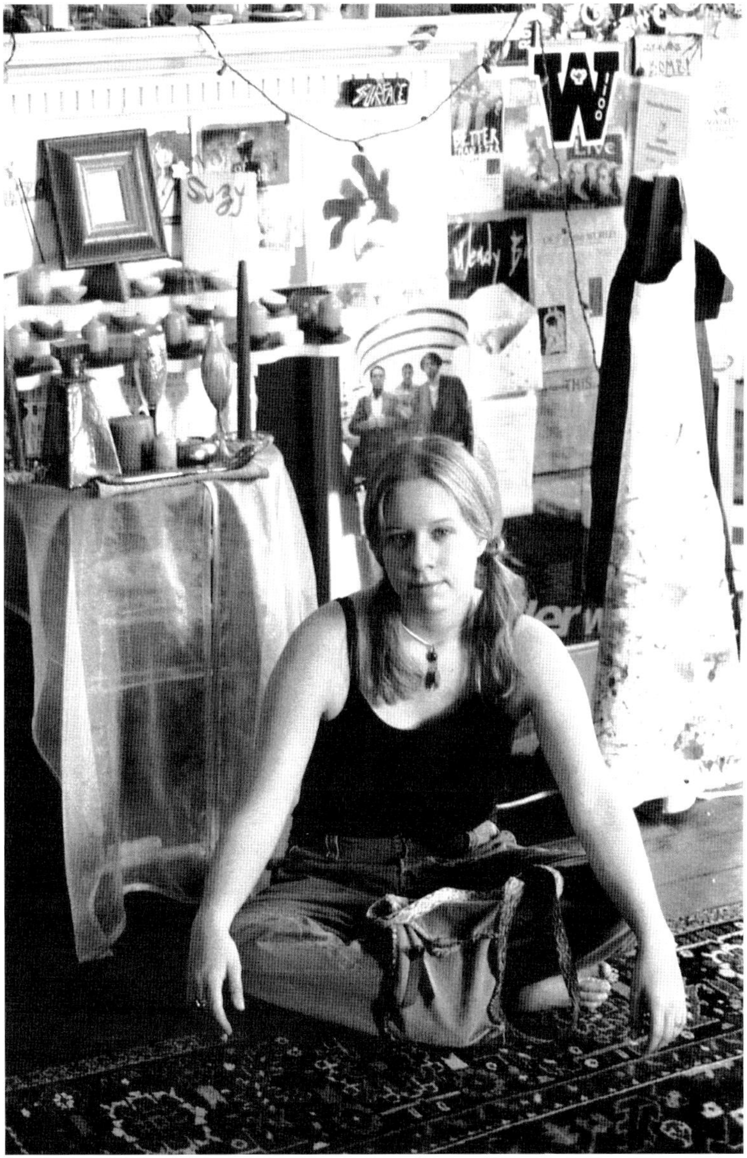
SURFACE
Suzy
W
LIVE

Anne Rivers Siddons

Novelist

Bottle Cap Purse

An artist made this purse, which I bought from an art gallery in Blue Hill, Maine. It's a perfect writer's purse, especially a shy writer. It works on a childish level and tells a wonderful story every time.

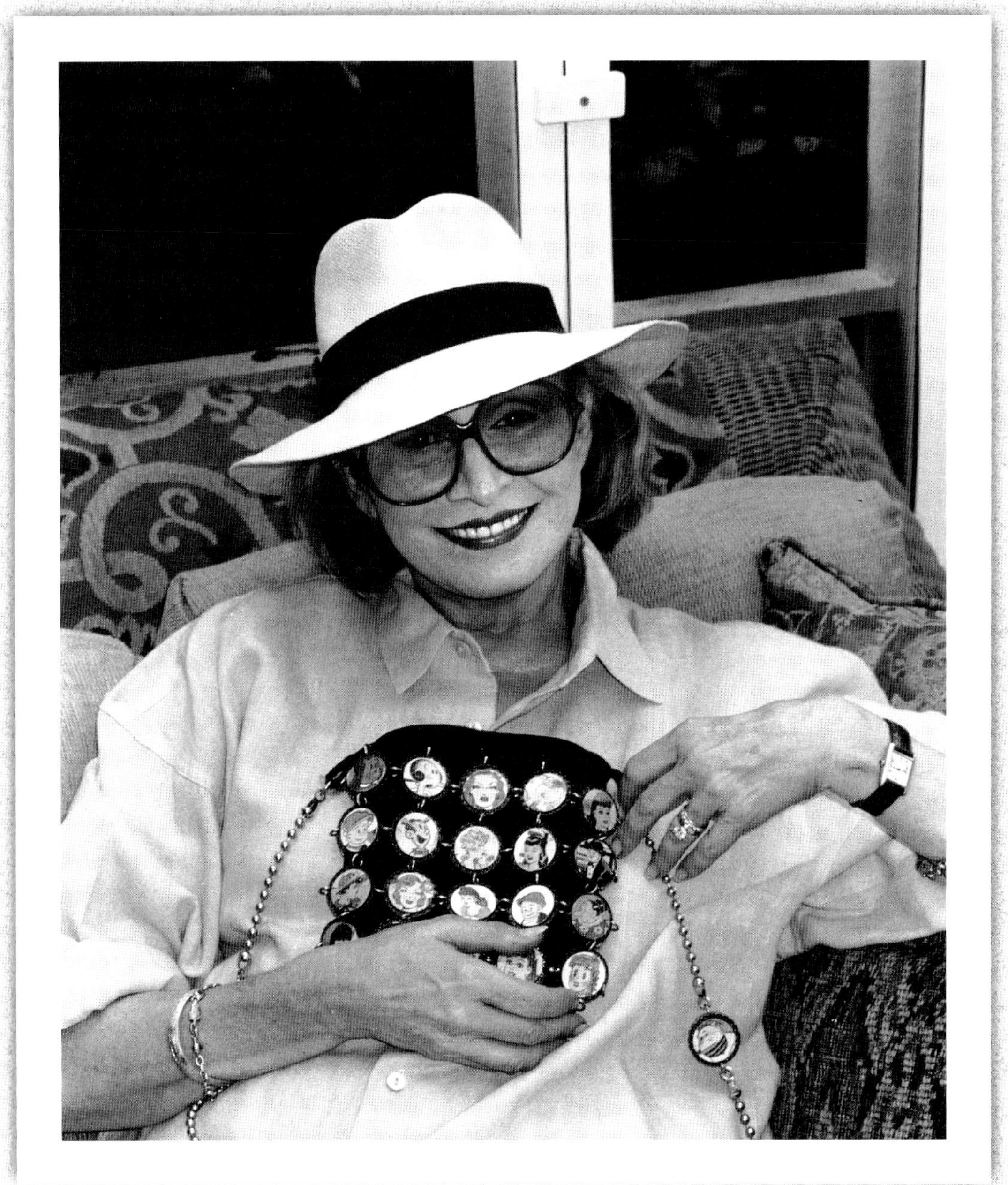

Jerri Chaplin
Poetry Therapist

Blue Jean Purse

This blue jean purse was made by a friend of mine who was Mrs. Hawaii in 1999. She is very artsy-craftsy. Using the denim as a canvas, she monogrammed it with my initials and embellished it with tokens, which symbolize the important things in my life. There's a tiny airplane, which stands for all the travel I do; a pair of sunglasses; shoes; and two little handbags.

Most meaningful is a miniature cluster of purple grapes, which represents Geffen, my older son. Geffen is Hebrew for grapevine. And there's a tiny angel to stand for Gabriel, my younger son.

I'm a Jewish mother, what can I tell you?

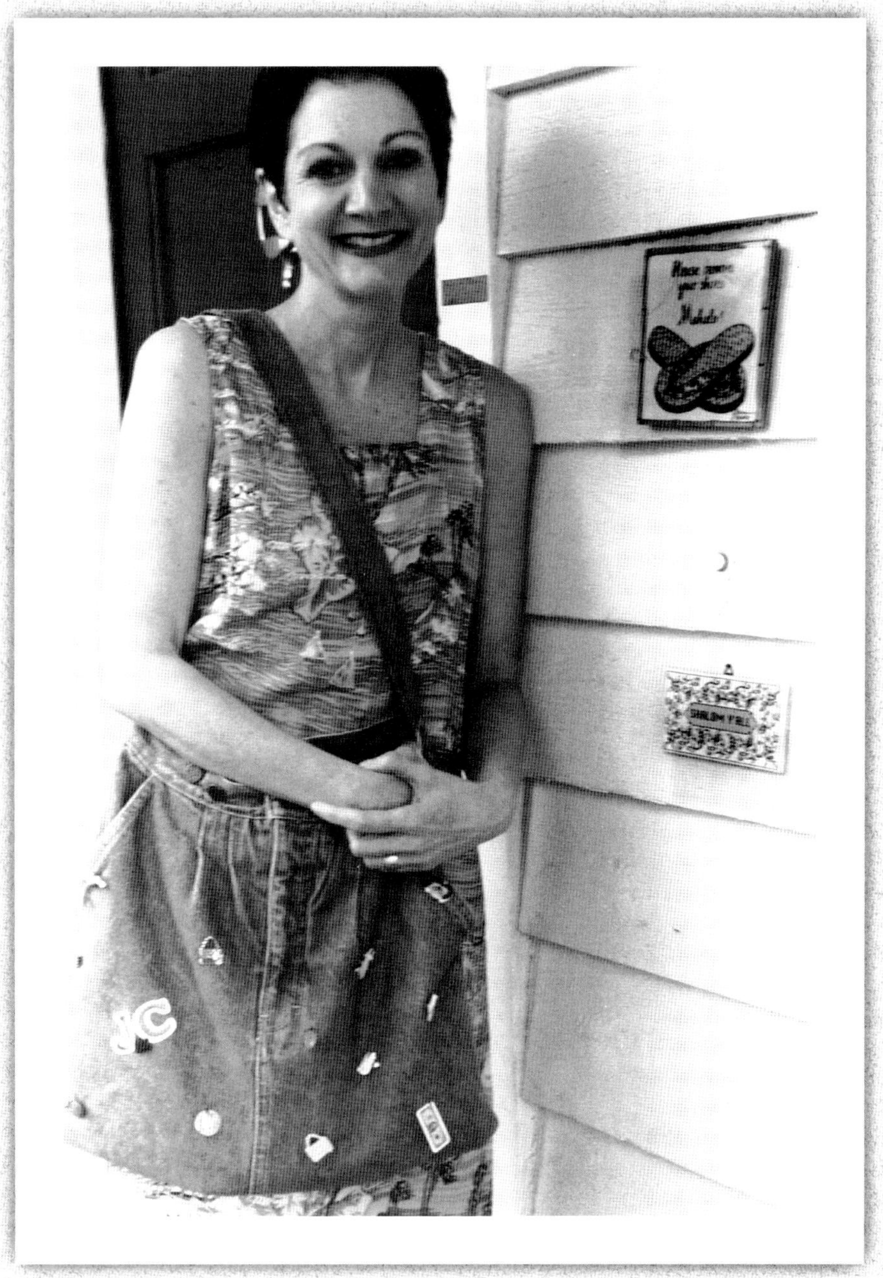

Hart Hagerty
Student

Sisal Bag from Market in Quintana Roo

I like it because . . . there is something about it. It's simple but it expresses me.

The purse is gray. I'm shy, so I identify with that. Yet there are all these colorful pinwheels on it. That expresses the loudness of me. It's scraggly. That expresses my laziness! It's kind of sloppily put together but creative, too. Artistic.

It was also inexpensive. My mom said I could have it.

My bag and I just befriended each other.

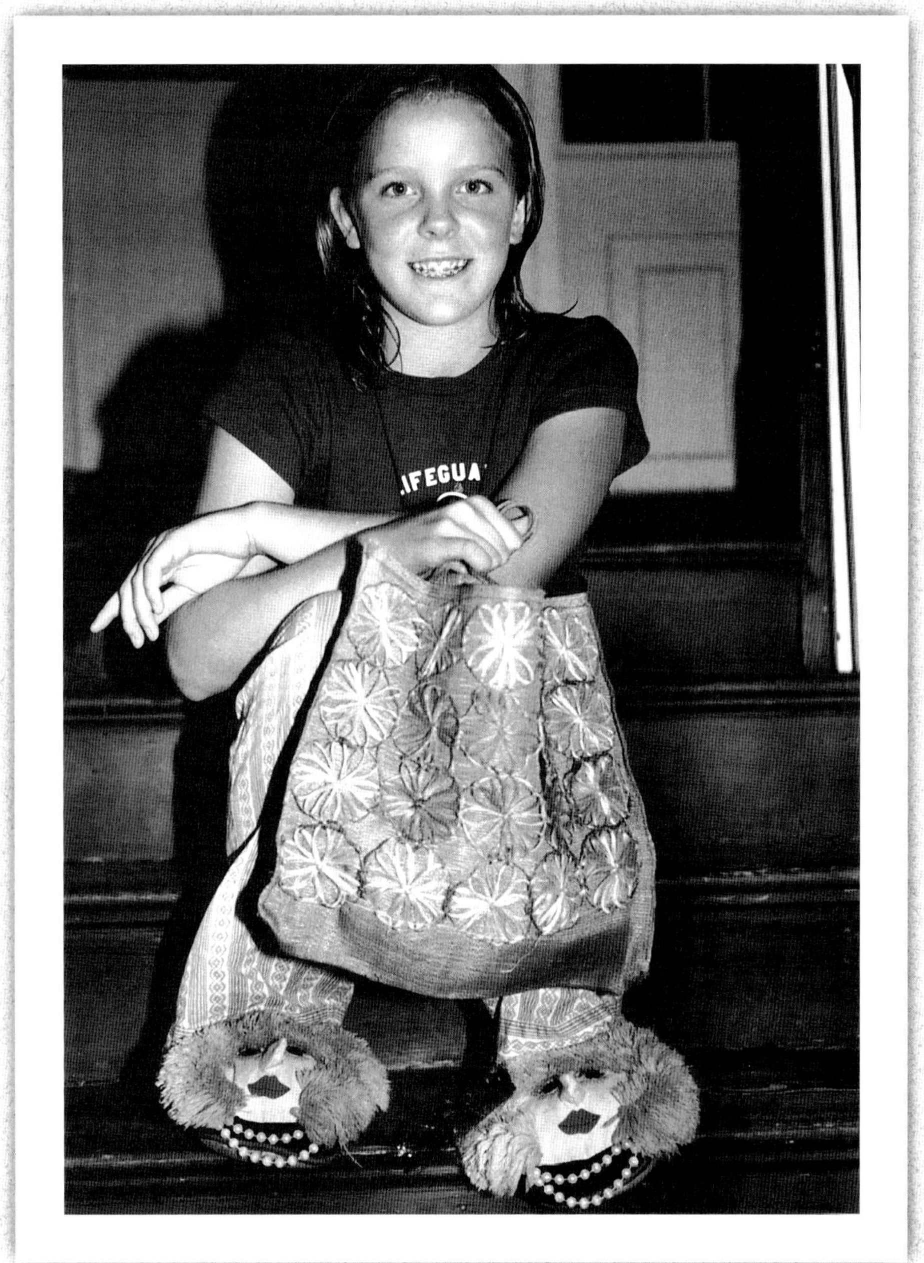

Lindsay Russell
Entrepreneur

Toile Purses

My name is Lindsay Russell, and I'm just beginning a handbag business named Etoile. My purses are made of toile material, which is French documentary linen picturing scenes of milkmaids milking, ladies swinging, couples courting in the French countryside.

Etoile is the French word for star. I love stars. I'm a bug freak. I love ferns. Anything tropical.

I've just taken the bold step of quitting my archaeology job to stay home and make as many purses as possible. Eek!

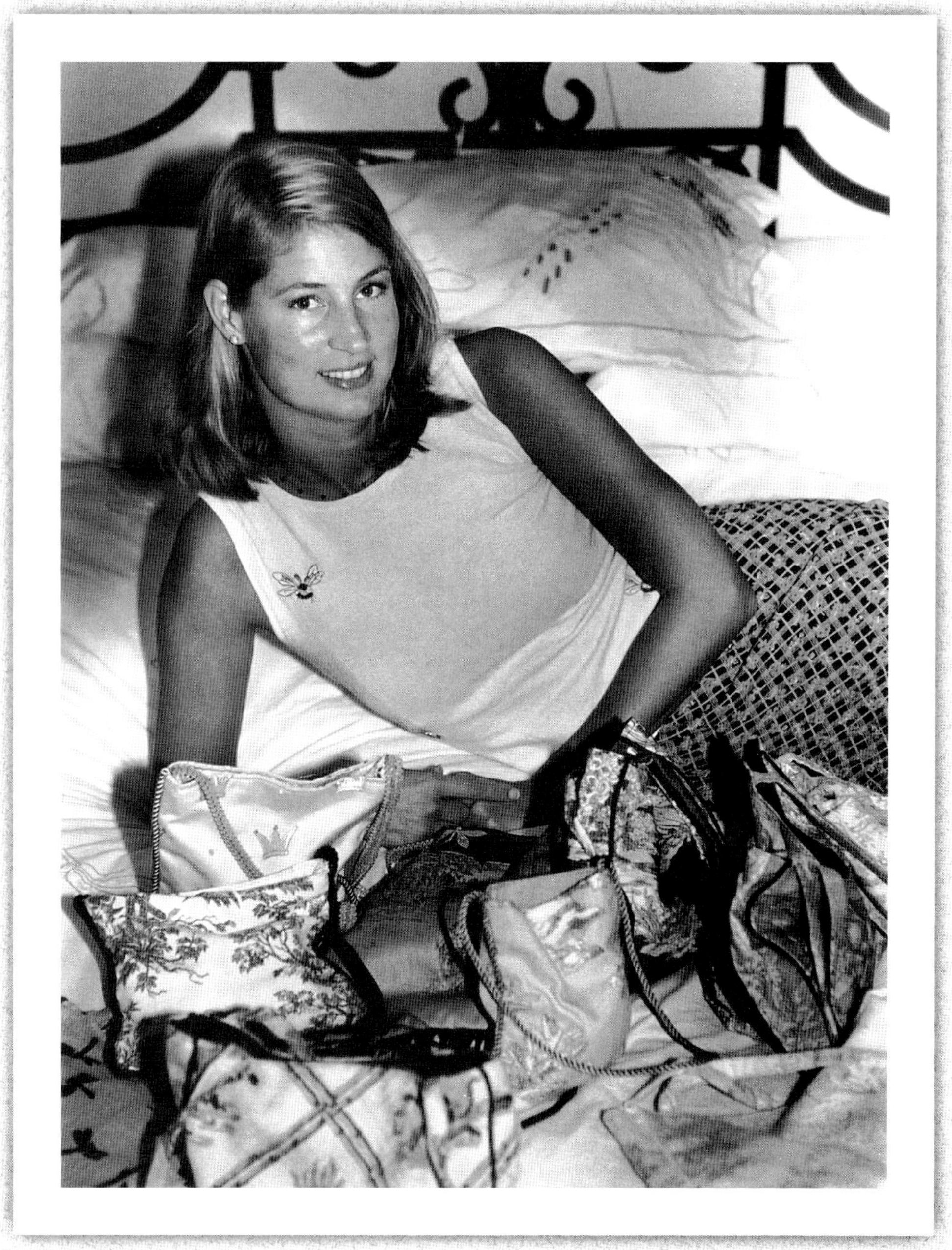

Lydia Evans
History Buff

Nantucket Purse

Nantucket basket purses are made of woven rattan with flat, wooden bottoms and ivory fittings. Their origins go back more than one hundred years, when Nantucket sailors made similar, larger ones to hold everything from blankets to fruit. The ivory tops are often customized to depict maps of the island, whales, seashells, or even the owner's home. My husband, Don, bought me one on a trip to New England.

I have always had a strong pull to New England. Dad's family, who are related to the Aldens, came to Massachusetts on the *Mayflower*, then moved to Vermont and the Midwest. I attended an Alden reunion at Duxbury, where John Alden built his house and had about ten children with Priscilla; descendants include John Adams, John Quincy Adams, Henry Wadsworth Longfellow, and the Delanos.

I chose a pair of scallops made of fossilized whale ivory for the top of my bag. At the time, I did not realize that the scallop is the Alden family symbol. That is just wild to me!

The Nantucket basket has survived the transition down to our age. When you go to the movie theater, you're squeamish about putting your purse on the floor, but it survives that and all other elements—the dust and grime—of our culture.

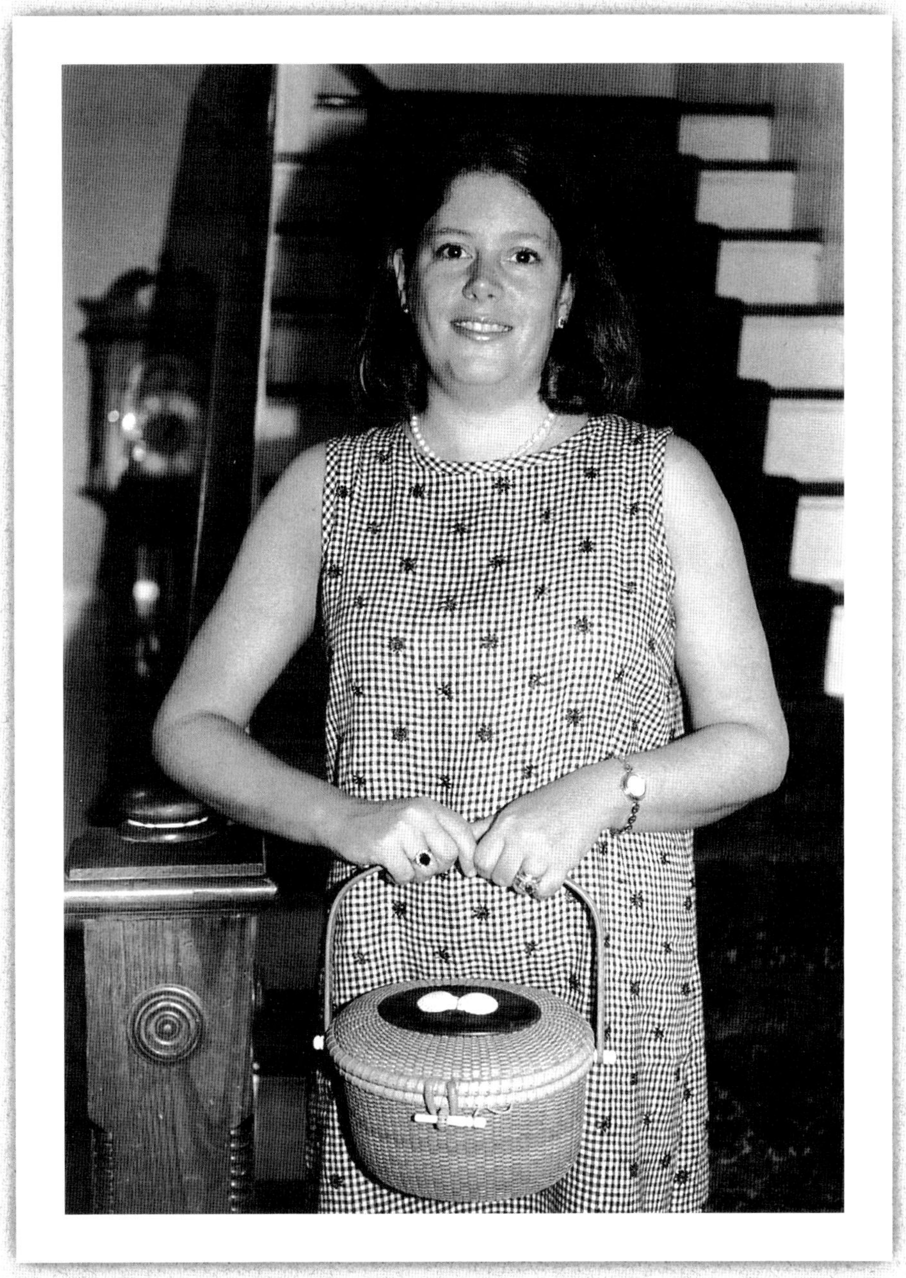

Alada Shinault-Small
a.k.a. Muima Maat
Artist, Performer

Multi-Compartmental Purse

Egypt used to be called Kamit, The Black Lands. In the Kamitic language, I am called Muima Maat, "One Who Flows With Others in the Essential Stream of Truth."

Just as my purse has many compartments, so does my life. I wear many hats: storyteller, dancer, choreographer, tour guide, teacher, and mommy. I keep rolling from one thing to the next, from doing library research to performing to wondering what the hell I am going to make for dinner.

With my accelerated lifestyle, having a purse with multiple compartments helps me keep my sanity. I'm never foraging for a business card. I know where it is. It's almost a Bob Barker thing. I know where my rubber bands, pencils, and paper clips are. I'm not digging like a gopher.

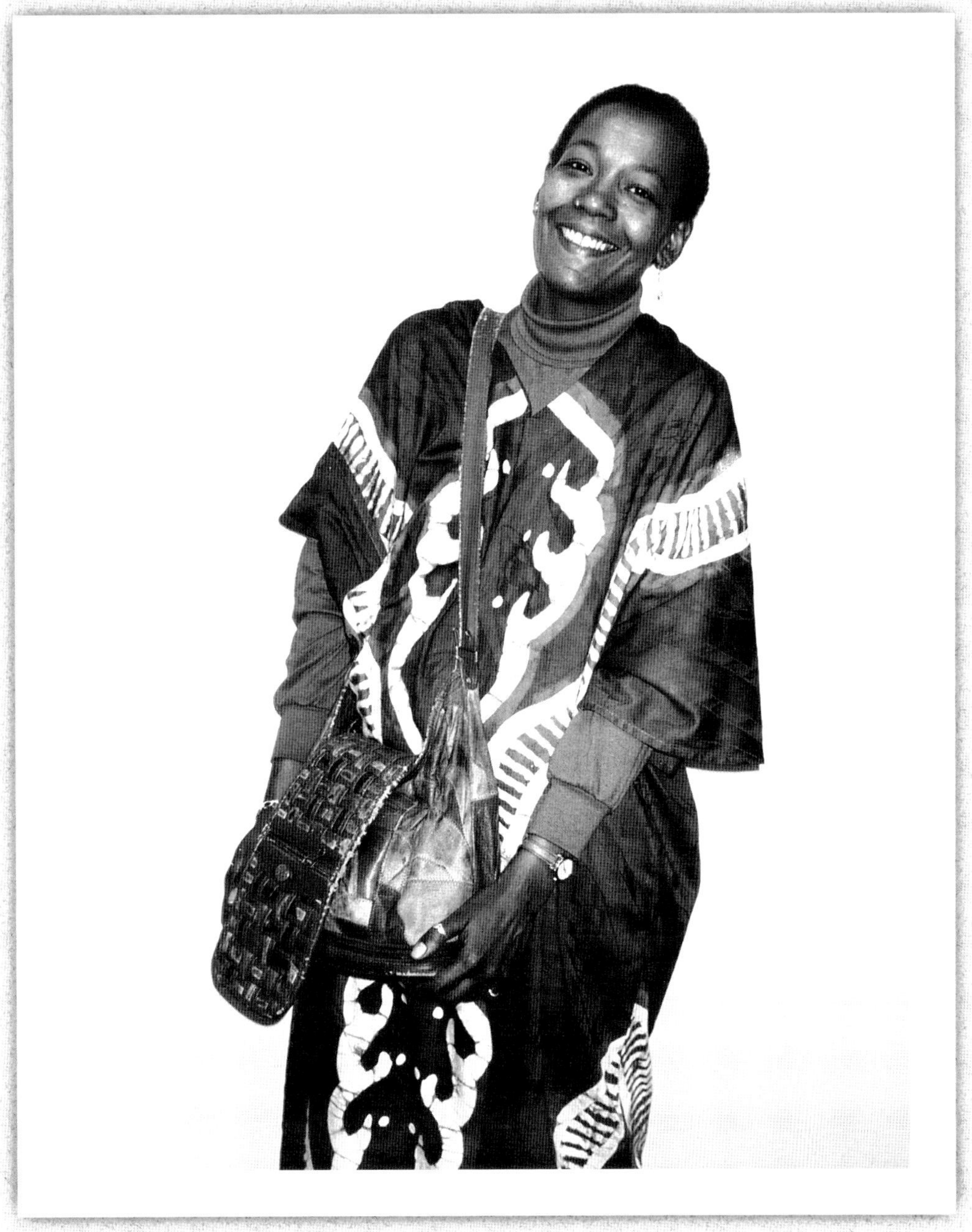

Jaime Hayes
Store Manager, Artist

Hippie-Granny Psychedelic Purse

I'm an artist. I paint in acrylics. It's all I can afford.

My purse is a little bit hippie, a little bit Granny, a little bit psychedelic. I've never seen another one like it. And it was only five dollars at the San Francisco Goodwill. It's unique just as I am unique. It's the perfect shape for holding books, and I always have one. Right now I'm reading *Tropic of Cancer* by Henry Miller.

The purse is open—no zippers, clasps, or Velcro. I don't have things I must undo that prevent me from getting to what I need. Likewise, I try to keep my mind open to new people and experiences.

I usually have my journal, organic rosewater, and a silver Chinese medicine ball in my purse. I keep my money in my pockets.

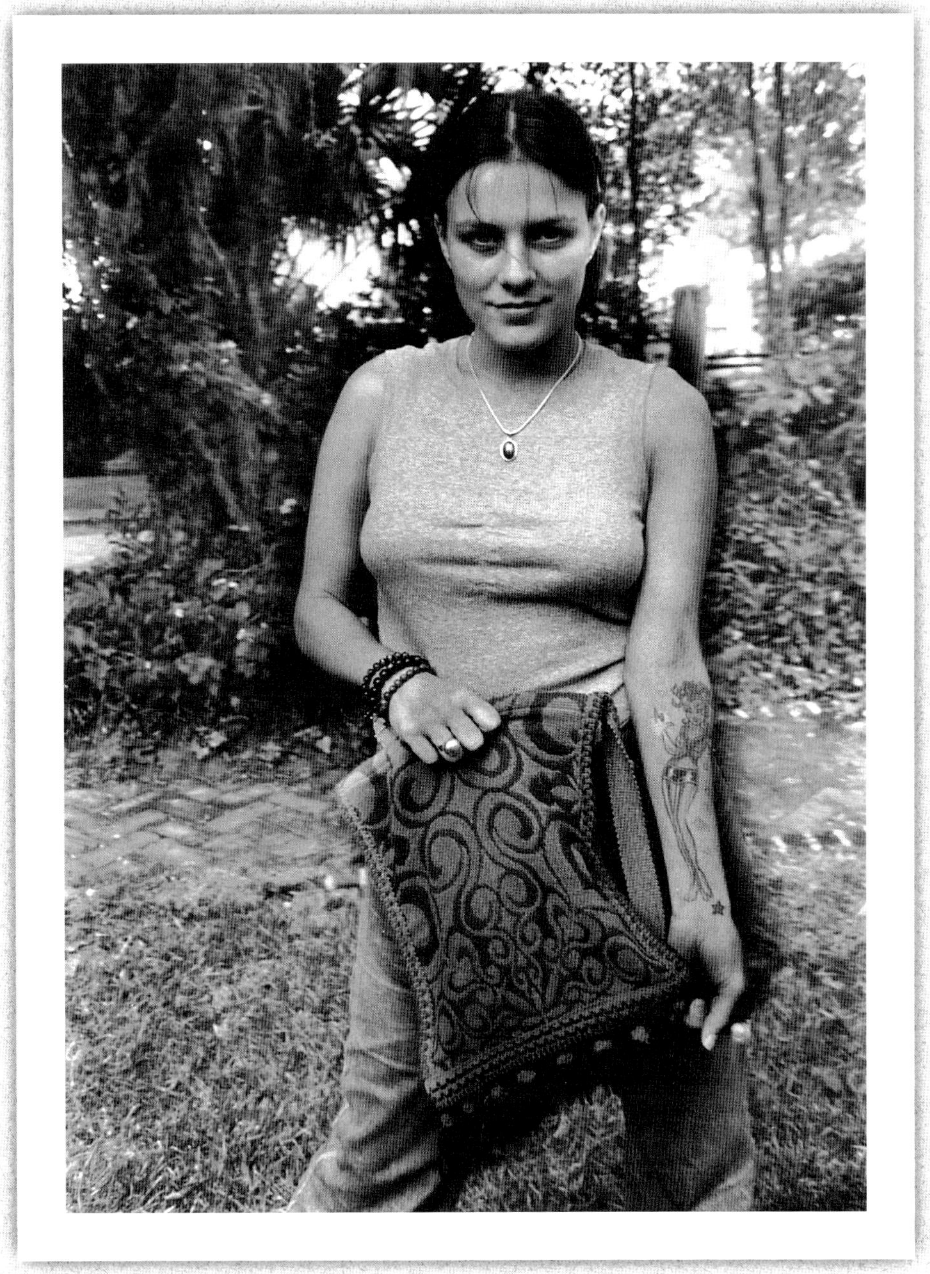

Lori Wyatt
Flight Attendant, Antiques Dealer

Vintage Purse

I think I was born at the wrong time. I love wearing vintage clothes, jewelry, and shoes when I'm not flying. I have a huge collection of old pocketbooks that I love to carry.

I appreciate the character, quality, workmanship and uniqueness of old, well-made things. You can reinvent yourself endlessly.

As a little girl, I played dress-up with my mother's dresses, high heels, and handbags. She had gorgeous handbags.

In a way, I've never stopped playing dress-up.

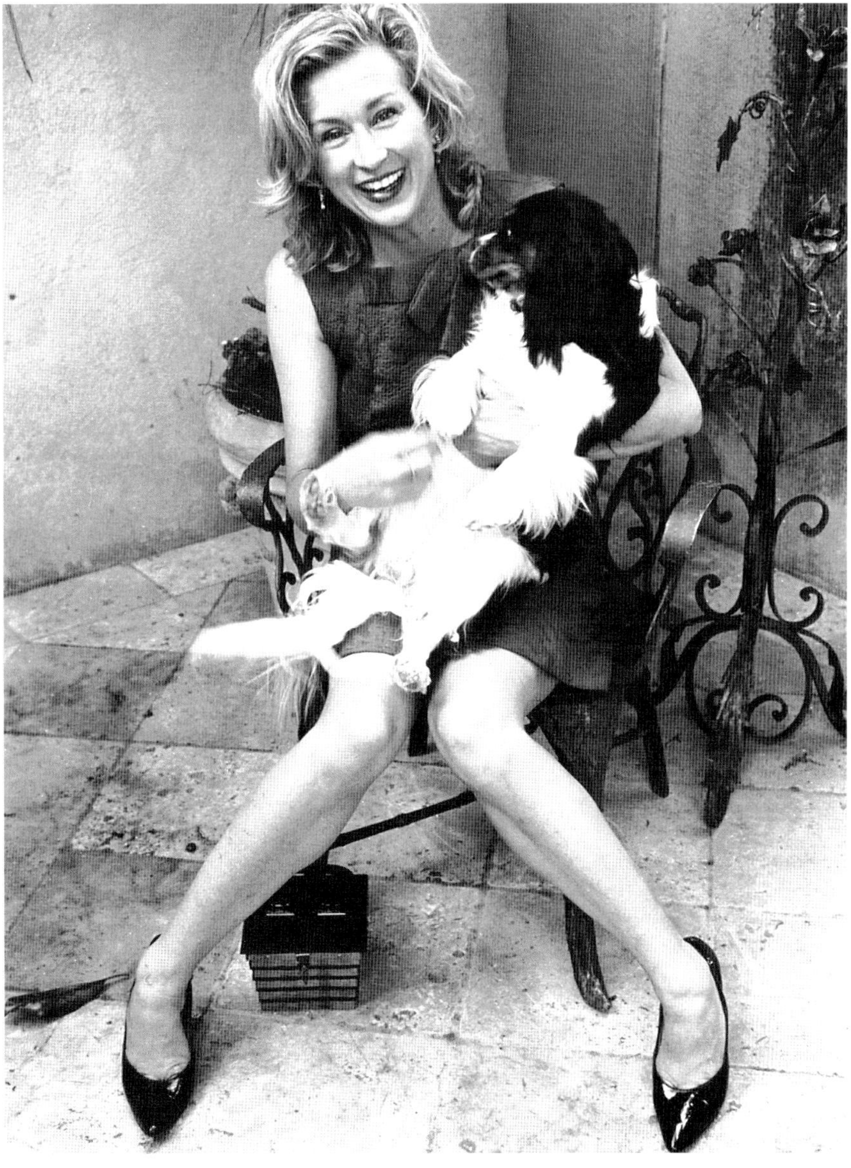

Sam Shirley
Tomboy

Clutch Purse

My real name is Dorothy, and I was born in Mt. Kisco, New York. I was a tomboy everyone called Butch. When I turned eleven, my dad changed my nickname to Sam because he thought Butch was just too unfeminine.

I started carrying clutch purses when I lived in Rome during the 1970s. I spoke fluent Italian and worked in a dress shop on the Via Veneto. Italian men loved to pinch and grab young girls, and I found a clutch purse useful for warding off unwelcome advances with a *whack*.

After Rome I headed south in a Winnebago with my mom. Everyone said, "Are you women crazy?" Our motor home was old and it broke down in South Carolina. Everyone was so friendly here we just stayed. I sold motor homes for thirteen years before starting a housecleaning business called Persnickety. My present husband, Larry, asked me to clean his house. We got married on Valentine's Day, 1998.

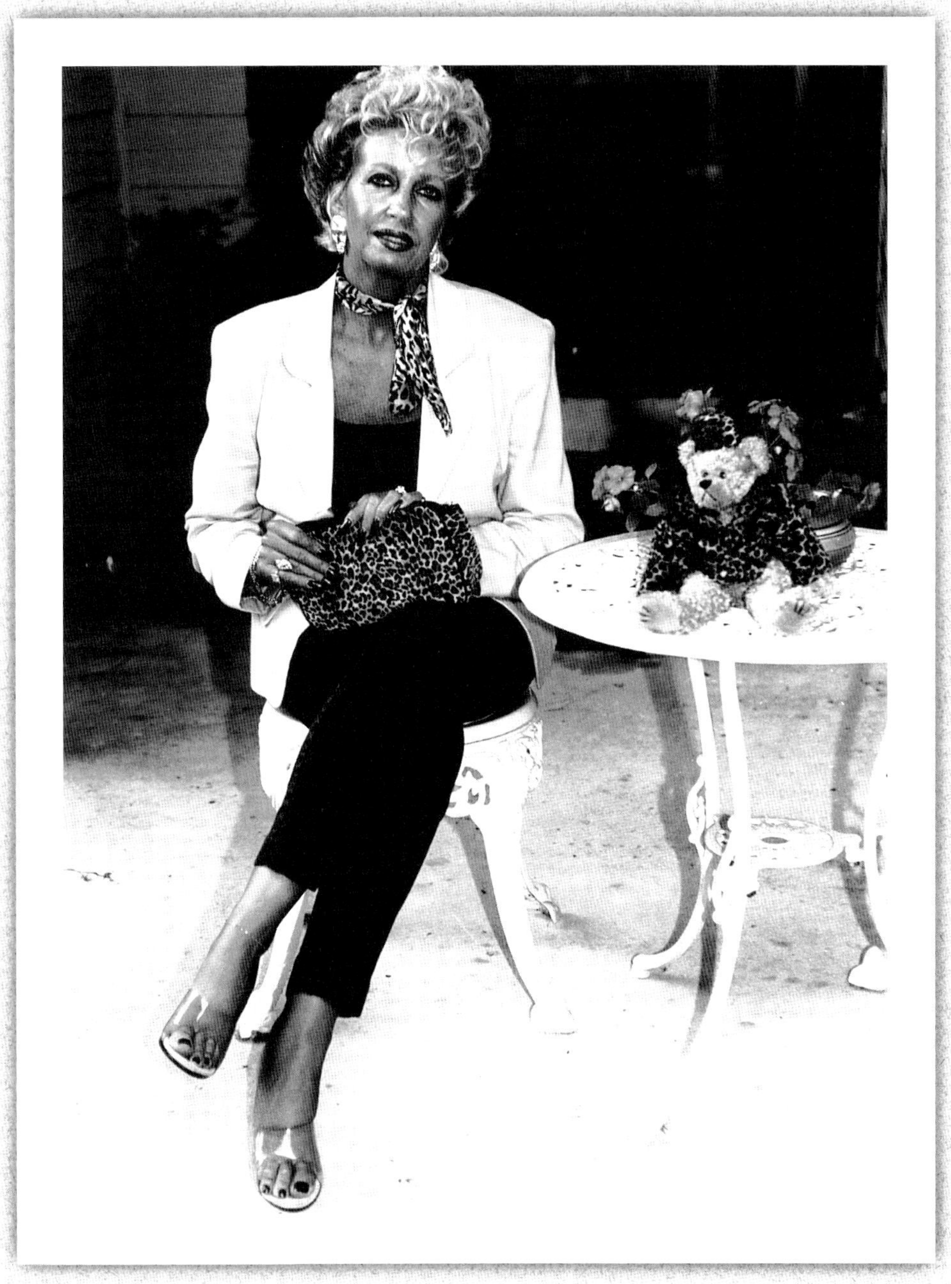

Marjory Wentworth
Poet

Endless Black Purse

My purse is merely a receptacle for the homeless pieces of paper I accumulate: Crumpled grocery lists and cash machine receipts fill the inside pockets, while expired coupons twirl around the pens. Even in the makeup bag, karate and baseball schedules separate the mascara and the lipstick from the Tampax and the Tylenol.

My purse is always black and big enough to hold the ordinary assortment of keys, loose change, pieces of chewing gum, Kleenex, Day-Timer, and the wallet with too many credit cards.

But somewhere beneath these day-to-day distractions, my endless black purse contains a not-so-ordinary marked-up draft of the poem I am passionately revising, which is folded into an ancient copy of Milton's *Paradise Lost*, long missing its cover and still smelling exactly like damp earth.

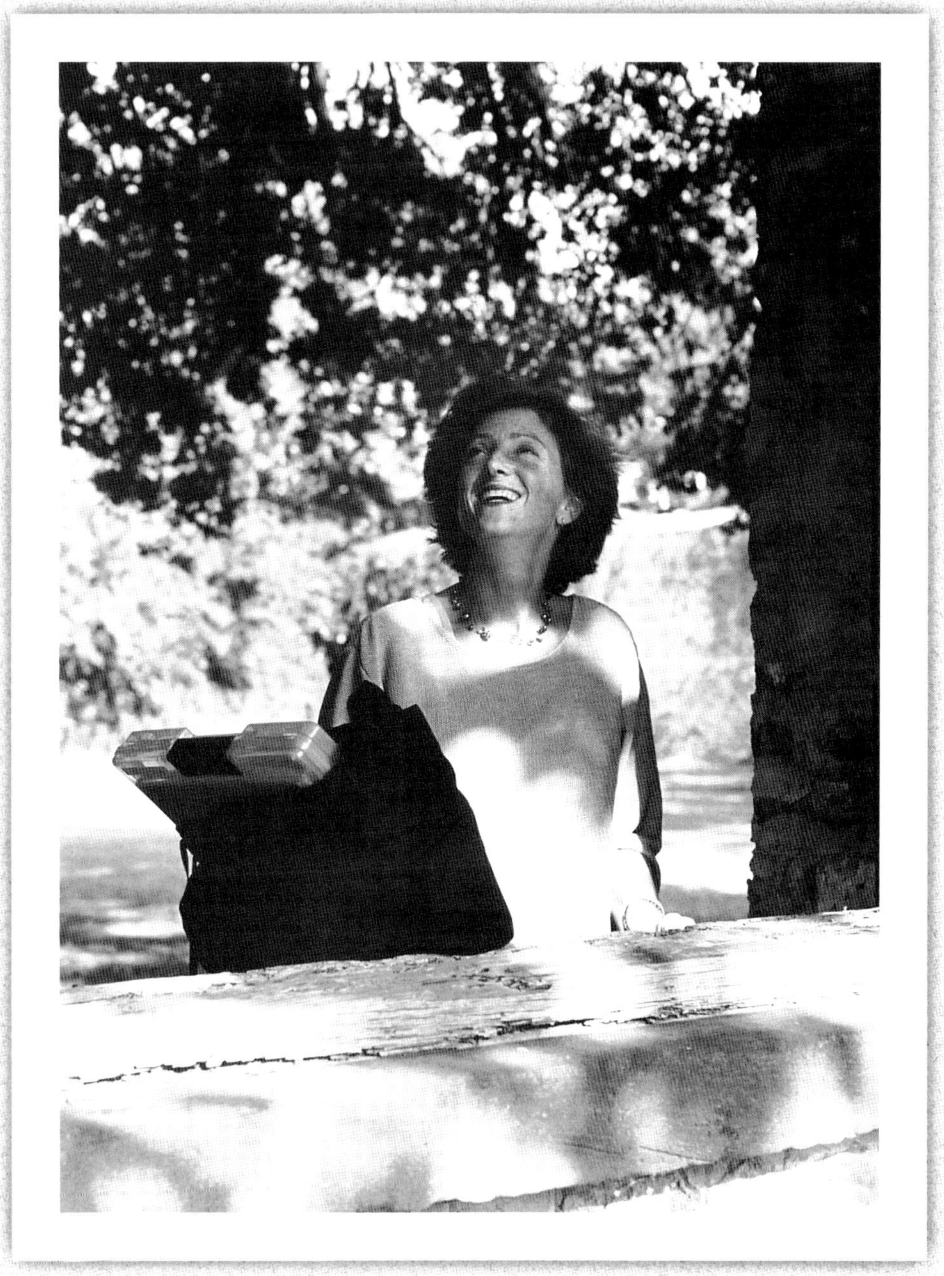

Christy Juckett
Graphic Designer

Cigar Box Purse

I like color. I put color in my paintings but prefer to dress in black and white. Maybe it's that I like fading into the background, the better to observe. I admire Kandinsky for his colors and Cézanne for his painterly style. I also like Dali, but it would scare me to paint that way.

In the 1950s there was a great production of box purses, which I appreciate for their shapes and handles. I started collecting cigar boxes from cigar stores. They are anywhere from free to five dollars. The nicer ones are made of cedar and often have compartments. I use one to store CDs, one for brushes, one for makeup.

It hit me one day to make a purse from a cigar box. I painted it white and added an ordinary door pull from the hardware store.

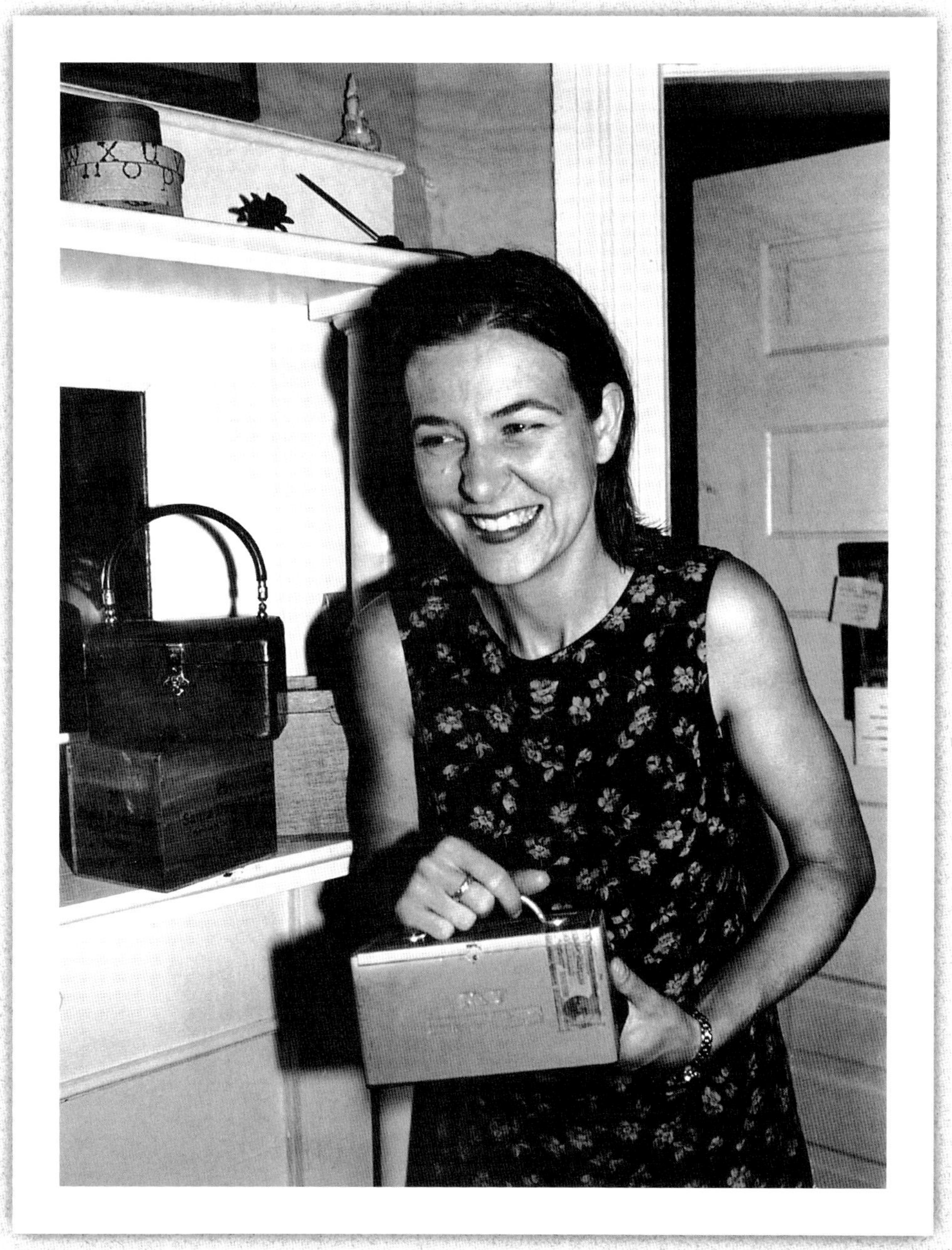

Ethel Greer

Grandmother

Sunday Purse

This is the purse I take with me on Sundays to the Union Baptist Church, where I have been a member for the past ten years. I bought it from the Avon lady.

Inside this purse I always have keys, credit cards, a lace handkerchief, money for the collection plate, and mints, lollipops, Lifesavers or gum for the little ones, so they won't fidget so much during the service.

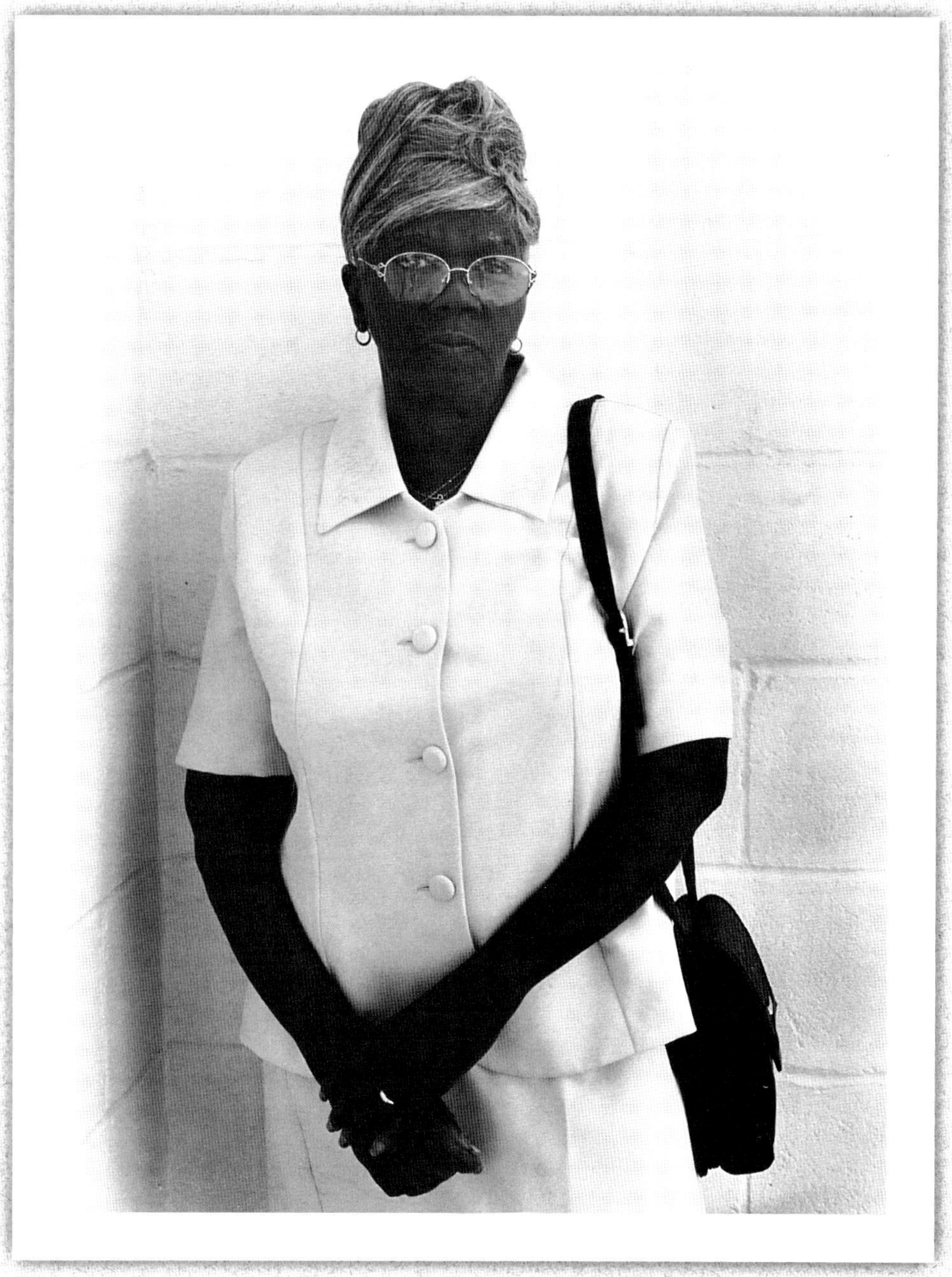

Barbara Julius

Jewelry Maker, Painter, Needlepointer

Bug Evening Purses

My inspiration came from Amy, who was my best fan. About seven years ago, we met in Oregon at a bed-and-breakfast. She had on a neat bracelet, and I said, "How do you do that?" We bought needle-nose pliers and she showed me. I taught her how to needlepoint. We spent the whole day with the light streaming in, designing, brainstorming, and drawing on our needlepoint scrims.

The next day the vacation was over. We dropped her off at Alamo Car Rental with a promise to get together three or four times a year. An hour later she crashed into a logging truck and died. Out there, they call that a "pancake" accident. Everything was flattened. Nothing survived but her scrim, which I made into a pillow for one of her daughters.

For weeks I was bereft. One day I started making jewelry. About that same time, the bug purses. I love insects for their intense colors and sparkle, like the ladybug and the dragonfly. I consider these purses like the jewelry Amy taught me to make—a form of radiant adornment.

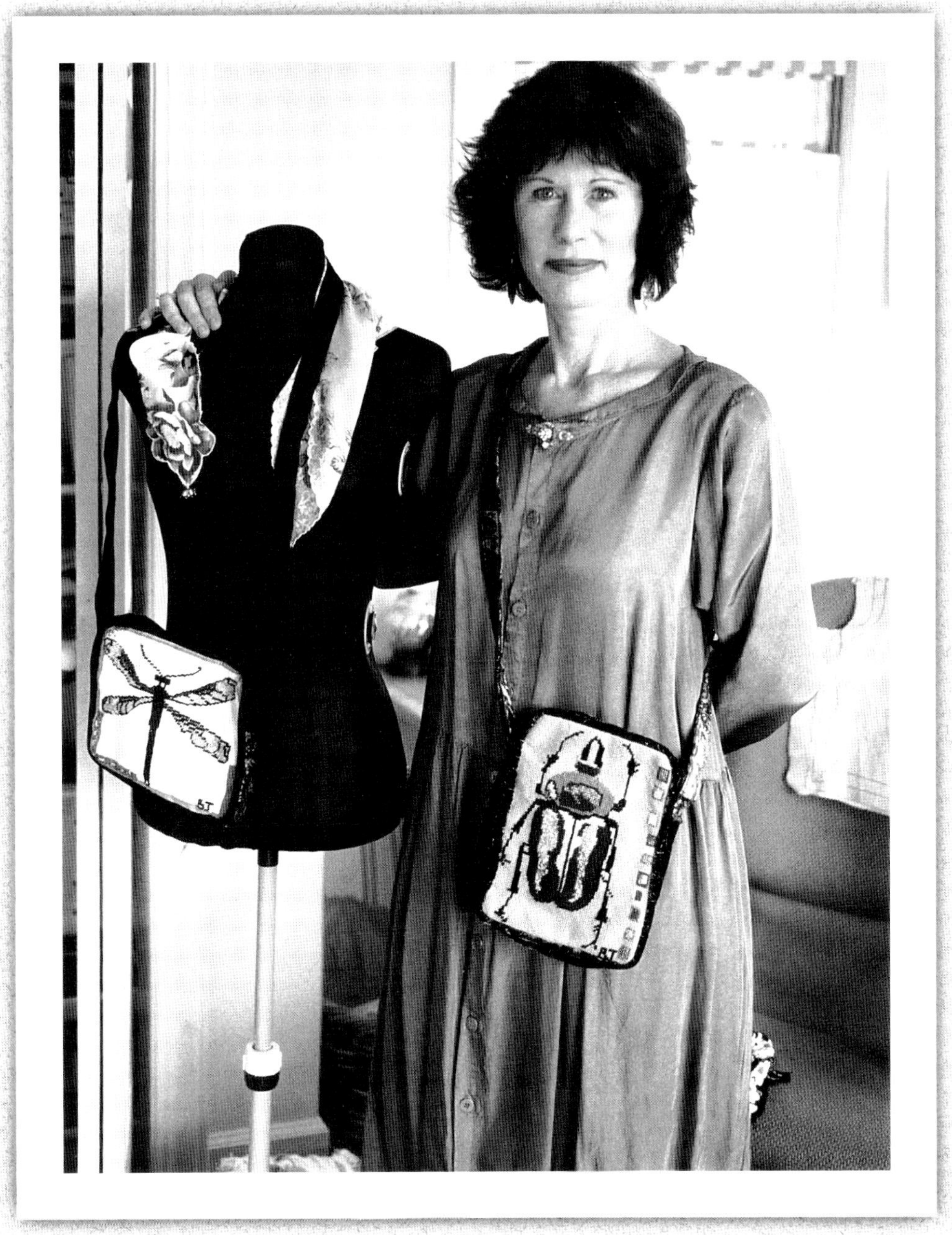

Margot Rose

Organizer

Efficiency Purse

In October 2000, my Day-Timer, calculator, and address book were retired. This Palm Pilot holds addresses, a date book, calculator, and memo pads. It records birthdays and due dates. I can track expenses on it or play solitaire.

I am organized. I came out of the womb that way. Even my CDs are in alphabetical order.

I also always have at least two of my favorite lipsticks with me. You never know when you are going to need to mix darker with light or flat with shimmery.

It's all about efficiency. With my lipsticks, Palm Pilot, and money in my purse, I'm ready to go.

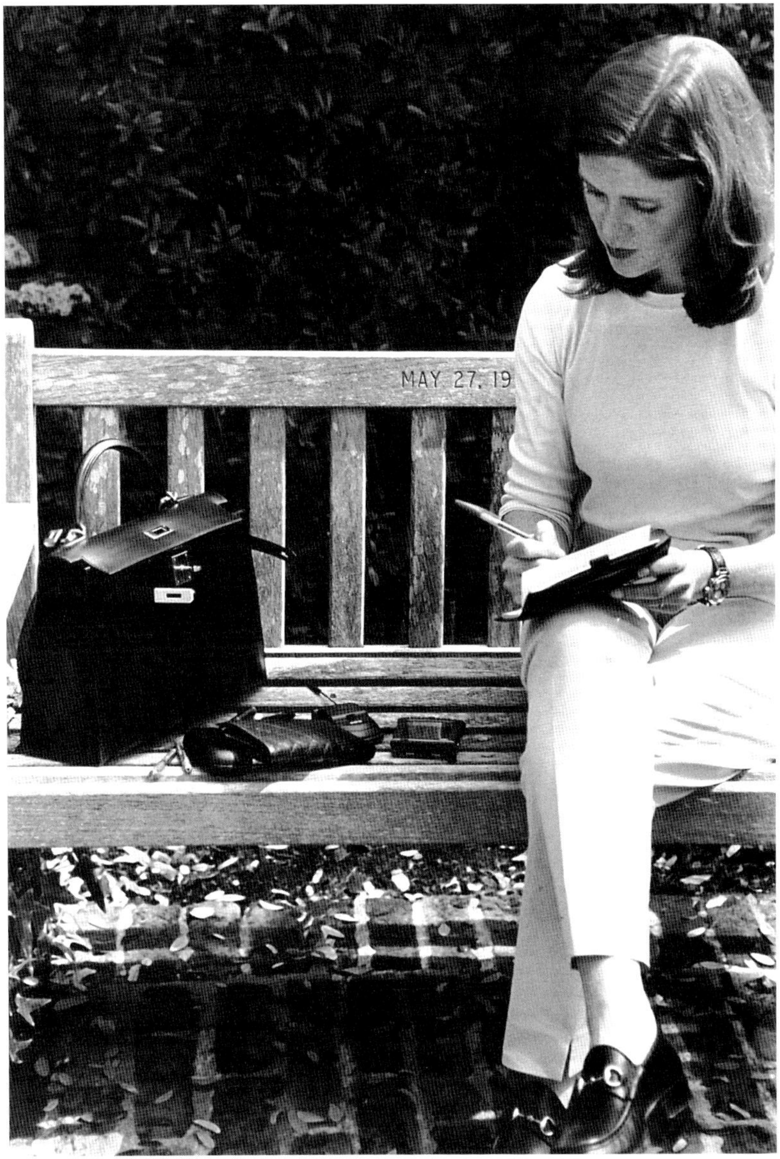
MAY 27, 19

Ellen E. Hyatt
Visiting Professor of English

Propriety Purse

My mother, Mae Mello, whose parents emigrated from Portugal, had a strong sense of boundaries and propriety, especially when it came to making others feel comfortable. She believed you should always watch the level of your voice, sit like a lady, and not overdo makeup. She was a stickler for good manners—especially thank you notes, which she believed should take some effort to compose. I used to love the sound of her fountain pen moving across paper as she wrote.

She used this purse mostly for church on Sunday and going out to dinner. It still contains her prayer book, a small scrap of fabric she intended to match for a sewing project, her folded pink Kleenex, and a small card picturing the Virgin Mary.

My mother died in 1985. When I use her purse, I'm reminded of her philosophy that you should always think about what you are doing and for what reason. There is a public persona to maintain. If I'm at home and yell "dammit" with only my cats to hear, that's one thing. If you are in public you must be aware you are sharing this time and space with others and be respectful.

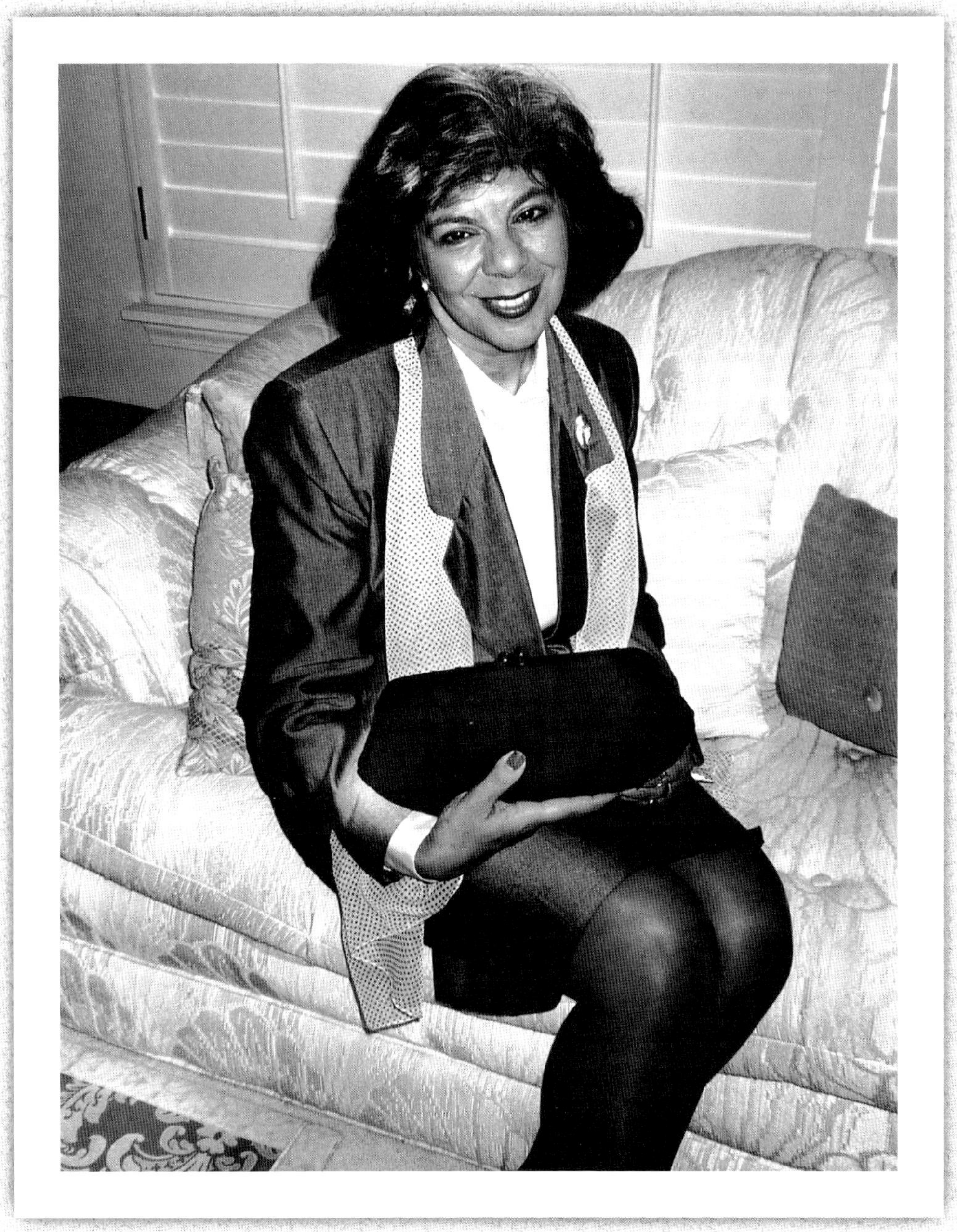

Purse Mysteries

This hidden tiny room
I carry
is formed of chambered hearts,
things held, withheld,
my longings and belongings.
It's an amulet on my arm,
little fetish,
small cave of secrets
held next to the body,
a sisterhood of sorts
—shield, lantern, talisman—
and each a friend, a story.

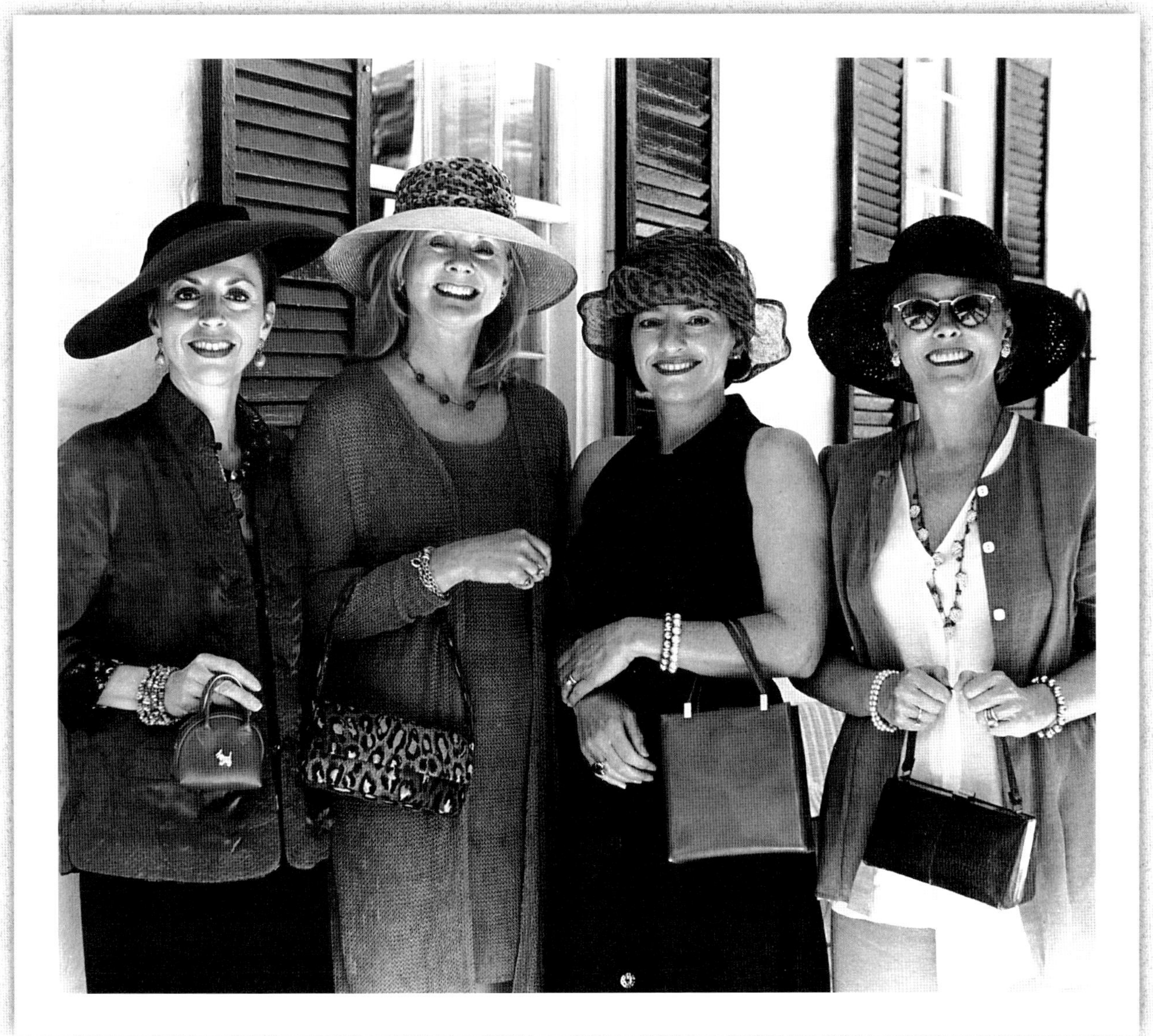

Acknowledgments

Myriad muses presided over the gestation of *Purse Universe.*

I'm grateful to Nikki Hardin, editor/publisher of *Skirt!*, for first publishing my portraits as "The Purse Project" in her cool pages. Sincere thanks also go to Anne and Heyward Siddons and to Ginger Barber for their friendship and enthusiasm.

To the Center for Women in Charleston; Oroton Handbags; Episcopal High School in Alexandria, Virginia; and to Charleston's Office of Cultural Affairs, I'm grateful for visual arts exhibitions of the portraits.

The Virginia Center for the Creative Arts provided a sanctuary for sustained work where I was fortunate to spend time last year.

I'm grateful to The South Carolina Arts Commission, which receives support from the National Endowment for the Arts, for awarding me an Artist's Project Grant in 1999–2000 to complete this work.

Special thanks go to Ellen Sullivan, Shelley DeLuca, and the hip crew at Crane Hill, and especially to Nina Costopoulos for her discerning eye.

More thanks go to family (two Richards, Gervais, Curry, and Hart), friends and colleagues: Ann Apple, Marti Atkins, Hilary Cadwallader, Sandi Mohlmann, Leslie Pelzer, Carolyn Rivers, Marge Wentworth, my Wednesday friends, Spencer Moore, Anne Pope, J.D. Cummings, Robin Stone, and John Kerr.

Finally, I thank the people in the portraits themselves. The relationship between photographer and subject is a reciprocal, egalitarian, and alchemical one. If *Purse Universe* reflects any of the light of our common humanity, as I hope it does, it shines from these generous people who opened themselves so freely to me.